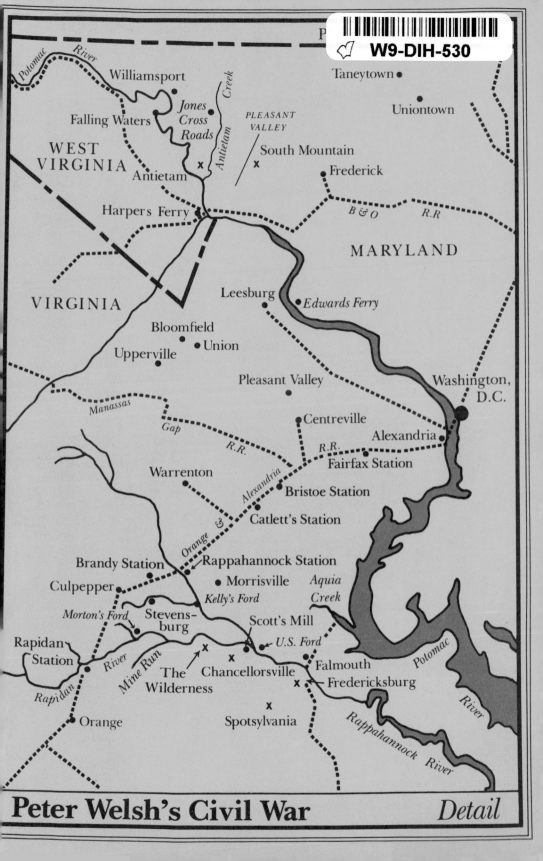

Peter Welsh's Civil War

Detail

IRISH GREEN
AND
UNION BLUE

PETER WELSH
in the dress uniform of an Irish Brigade sergeant
Photo: R. A. Lewis, 152 Chatham Street, New York City, ca. March 1864

"IRISH GREEN
AND
UNION BLUE"

THE CIVIL WAR LETTERS OF
PETER WELSH
COLOR SERGEANT
28TH REGIMENT
MASSACHUSETTS VOLUNTEERS

Edited by
LAWRENCE FREDERICK KOHL
with
MARGARET COSSÉ RICHARD

New York
FORDHAM UNIVERSITY PRESS
1986

PUBLICATION OF THIS BOOK
WAS MADE POSSIBLE IN PART BY A GRANT FROM
THE HARRY J. SIEVERS, S.J. MEMORIAL PUBLISHING FUND

Printed in the United States of America

CONTENTS

THE LETTERS

Illustrations between pages 106 and 107
Maps endpapers

ABBREVIATIONS AND SHORT TITLES

Appletons' Cyclopaedia

Appletons' Cyclopaedia of American Biography (New York: Appleton, 1888).

Athearn, *Meagher*

Robert G. Athearn, *Thomas Francis Meagher: An Irish Revolutionary in America* (Boulder: University of Colorado Press, 1949).

Boatner, *Dictionary*

Mark Mayo Boatner III, *The Civil War Dictionary* (New York: McKay, 1959)

Catton, *Army of the Potomac*

Bruce Catton, *The Army of the Potomac*, 3 vols., I: *Mr. Lincoln's Army*; II: *Glory Road*; III: *A Stillness at Appomattox* (Garden City, N.Y.: Doubleday, 1951–53).

Conyngham, *Irish Brigade*

D. P. Conyngham, *The Irish Brigade* (New York: McSorley, 1867).

DAB

Dictionary of American Biography, 20 vols., Index, Suppls. (New York: Scribners, 1928–).

Fox, *Regimental Losses*

William F. Fox, *Regimental Losses in the American Civil War, 1861–1865* (Albany: Albany Publishing Co., 1889).

Germain, *Catholic Chaplains*

Aidan Henry Germain, *Catholic Military and Naval Chaplains, 1776–1917* (Washington, D.C., 1929).

Hernon, *Celts*

Joseph M. Hernon, Jr., *Celts, Catholics & Copperheads: Ireland Views the American Civil War* (Columbus: Ohio State University Press, 1968).

Livermore, *Numbers & Losses*

Thomas L. Livermore, *Numbers & Losses in the Civil War in America: 1861–65* (Bloomington: Indiana University Press, 1957).

Long, *Civil War Day by Day*

E. B. Long, *The Civil War Day by Day: An Almanac, 1861–1865* (Garden City, N.Y.: Doubleday, 1971).

Lord, *They Fought for the Union*

Francis A. Lord, *They Fought for the Union* (Harrisburg, Pa.: Stackpole, 1960).

Mass. Adj.-Gen.

Massachusetts, Adjutant-General, *Annual Report of the Adjutant-General of the Commonwealth of Massachusetts* (Boston: Wright and Potter).

Mass. Soldiers

Massachusetts, Adjutant-General, *Massachusetts Soldiers, Sailors, and Marines in the Civil War*, 8 vols. (Norwood, Mass.: Norwood Press, 1931–35).

Mass. Volunteers

Massachusetts, Adjutant-General, *Record of the Massachusetts Volunteers, 1861–1865*, 2 vols. (Boston: Wright & Potter, 1868–70).

Mass. War Records

Commonwealth of Massachusetts, Military Division, War Records Research, Natick, Massachusetts

NA

National Archives, Washington, D.C.

OR

The War of the Rebellion: A Compilation of the Official Records of the Union and Confederate Armies, 128 vols. (Washington, D.C.: Government Printing Office, 1880–1902).

Phisterer, *New York in the War*

Frederick Phisterer, ed., *New York in the War of the Rebellion, 1861–1865,* 5 vols. and index, 3rd ed. (Albany: Lyon, 1912).

Wiley, *Billy Yank*

Bell Irvin Wiley, *The Life of Billy Yank: The Common Soldier of the Civil War* (Indianapolis: Bobbs–Merrill, 1952).

EDITORIAL NOTE

In order to preserve their distinctive character, the letters are published here virtually as written. The only alterations made are those required for typographical clarity. Thus, where Peter Welsh tended to run his text together, to take full advantage of scarce pieces of paper, the editor has added extra space to break up his unpunctuated sentences. The arrangement of the salutation and close is also an accommodation to accepted format, and the very few editorial interpolations are clearly indicated by brackets. Where brief passages from the letters are quoted in the Preface, the Introduction, or other editorial matter, their spelling and punctuation have been regularized, so as not to impede the narrative flow.

ACKNOWLEDGMENTS

Indebtedness to many arouses fear of overlooking some whose help has been significant; yet the risk must be taken, for this work could not have been completed without the generous assistance of the following librarians, archivists, and other professionals.

Daniel W. Bennett III, Otis Historical Archives, Armed Forces Medical Museum, Washington, D.C.

Mary E. Braney, Commonwealth of Massachusetts State Library, Boston.

Joseph J. Casino, Ryan Memorial Library, St. Charles Academy, Philadelphia.

Richard M. Cochran, University of Notre Dame, Notre Dame, Indiana.

James E. Fahey, Commonwealth of Massachusetts, Military Division, War Records Research, Natick.

R. E. Feeney, Commonwealth of Massachusetts, Military Division, War Records, Adjutant General's Office, Boston.

Steven Hill, Newark, Delaware.

Nicholas de Jong, Public Archives, Charlottetown, Prince Edward Island, Canada.

Library of Congress, Photoduplication Service, Washington, D.C.

Michael J. McAfee, United States Military Academy Museum, West Point, New York.

Collin MacDonald, Centreville, Virginia.

Howard Madaus, Milwaukee Public Museum, Milwaukee, Wisconsin.

National Museum of American History, Smithsonian Institution, Washington, D.C.

New York Genealogical and Biographical Society, New York City.

New York Public Library, Map Room Research Staff, New York City.

Jimmy B. Parker, Genealogical Department, Church of Jesus Christ of Latter-Day Saints, Salt Lake City, Utah.

George Ryan, *The Pilot*, Boston.

Jerry M. Sagliocca, Bureau of War Records, New York State Division of Military and Naval Affairs, Albany.

Larry Sullivan, Jan Anderson, and Katherine Richards, New-York Historical Society, New York City.

Ross Urquhart, Massachusetts Historical Society, Boston.

Robert M. Warner, National Archives and Record Service, Washington, D.C.

Kevin Whelan, The National Library of Ireland, Dublin.

Paul R. White, Jr., National Archives, Boston Branch, Waltham, Massachusetts.

Michael J. Winey, U. S. Army Military History Institute, Carlisle Barracks, Pennsylvania.

Anthony Zito, The Catholic University of America, Washington, D.C.

Preface

MARGARET COSSÉ RICHARD

HOW THE LETTERS SURVIVED

THE LETTERS Peter Welsh wrote to his wife Margaret from the camps and battlefields of the Civil War are a powerful testimonial to man's all-consuming quest for freedom. Inscribed on fragile paper of varying size, the letters were preserved by his wife in a Victorian writing case, its red leather showing the ravages of 122 years or more of handling and confinement in a storeroom trunk. Most of the letters are written in ink.

The words are alive. They stir the hearts of those who read them. And they are the measure of the man whose heritage was the culmination of oppression, famine, and persecution in Ireland—a man whose dream was America!

Along with her husband's letters, Margaret kept letters Peter wrote to other members of the family, especially relatives in Ireland, if their letters had been sent to her for forwarding, and if, in so doing, she had persuaded the recipients to return them to her for safekeeping. In this way she managed to obtain the fine, long letter Peter wrote to his wife's father, another to her brother, and one seemingly undated and unaddressed on the subject of Negroes in the army. As the letters came they were carefully folded into her writing case to be withdrawn for frequent reading during passing years.

Found also among the letters are military documents that identify the time and place of Peter's birth and church records that certify to his marriage, but the twenty-seven years between these two significant events escaped the archivists. Where the soldier was schooled is unknown today, yet his letters leave no doubt that he was literate.

After the war the soldier's widow made her home in New York with the family of her younger sister, Mrs. Michael Joseph Hoey,

xiii

the former Sarah Prendergast. Sarah and Michael named their first daughter Margaret in tribute to Margaret Prendergast Welsh, who became then, and remained thereafter, lovingly Aunt Marda. When she died in April 1892, her precious letters survived in the care of her sister, who later entrusted them to my mother.

Now I, co-editor of the Peter Welsh letters and a descendant of the soldier through my grandmother Sarah Prendergast Hoey, and her daughter, my mother Margaret Hoey Cossé, share them in this book with all who may be interested.

The original letters, together with military and other documents preserved with them, are to be placed after publication for safe-keeping in the archives of The New-York Historical Society.

THE MAN PETER
AS THE FAMILY REMEMBERS HIM

Relatives today revere the memory of Peter Welsh, a memory gleaned both from family lore and from his letters to his wife, Margaret, while he was serving in the Union Army during the Civil War.

Above all, the family remembers Peter as a deeply dedicated patriot, a man of unswerving faith in God, who saw the Civil War as the first test of a modern free government in a struggle to defend itself, and a man who knew what he had to do to help preserve the union. In enlisting in September 1862, Peter Welsh determined his own destiny as he swore that he would "bear true faith and allegiance to the United States of America," and that he would "serve them honestly and faithfully against all their enemies whom-soever." And in the same document the recruiting officer certified "on honor" that Peter Welsh "when enlisted was entirely sober and duly qualified to perform the duties of an able-bodied soldier."[1]

From that point on, Peter's letters and military documents comprise virtually the only record of his life. The letters are never mere romantic effusions. Instead they are the outpouring of a caring husband, patient in responding to his wife's "frettings," modestly descriptive of battles, never dwelling on the grotesque, but intellectually and philosophically revealing of the man—a simple man, a carpenter, but a man of heroic character.

True, the soldier's knowledge of history, the Bible, and current events heighten the interest of scholars in these letters, but the family cherishes as well other attributes that shine through the collection.

For example there is his loyalty. After the debacle of Fredericksburg, he wrote to his wife that "I remained until dark, and then brought out some wounded belonging to our company," and further that "I went over the battlefield again before daylight to see if I could find any more of our men."[2] Still further, "I have sworn to serve faithfully and with God's blessing I will keep that oath,"[3] or in another letter, "This is my country as much as that of any man that was born on the soil, and so it is with every man who comes to this country and becomes a citizen."[4]

And there is his pride. On one occasion he told his wife there was no other soldier in Company K who could estimate and distribute rations properly. "They do not know," he said, "how to figure up the amount a given number of men should draw, so I keep account and see that we get the proper allowance."[5] Another time he assured Margaret that "you need not be afraid of me being reduced in rank. I never got into any trouble nor got into any disgrace, nor received a single reprimand from an officer."[6]

And a most important quality to the family is Peter's Catholicism. Repeatedly in his letters he expresses his faith in God. And each time he fought in a devastating battle, and could report to his wife that he "came out safe," his faith was reinforced. He expressed delight when his regiment was joined with the Irish Brigade because the brigade had three chaplains. He now had frequent opportunity to attend mass and evening prayers, and to avail himself of the sacraments. So secure was he in his faith, Peter could tell his wife: "Being separated from you for so long is the only worldly care or trouble I have."[7]

That Peter loved his wife is evidenced throughout the letters, but never more touchingly than when Margaret failed to share his ecstasy on being appointed to carry the green flag of Erin. In fact, he was dismayed when she, sensing the danger of his new assignment, urged him to resign the honor. "I can't believe you would suggest such a cowardly act,"[8] he told her, yet his devotion to Margaret and patience in responding to her "frettings" led, not to resentment, but to an explanation of how much safer he believed he would be with the flag than elsewhere in the ranks.

Peter's talent as a carpenter was constantly in demand, erecting camp quarters, improvising chapels or banquet halls, even constructing coffins "out of pieces of boxes."[9]

In May 1863 when the camp was moved, Peter wrote to Margaret that "I have got the purtyest little shanty in this company. I built it for myself and the first sergeant. I also built one for our captain. All the officers are trying to get up ones like this."[10] And he was always glad to help them.

Another quality cherished by the family is Peter's sobriety. Knowing, of course, that it was a "spree," born of frustration and followed by remorse, that led to his enlistment, Margaret worried about her husband's obtaining liquor in the army. But Peter, boasting of improved health, told his wife that he no longer felt any of the "nasty weakness" that came over him when he was working indoors and made him "crave" a stimulant. In short, he said, "I do not care for it now."[11]

And finally, Peter's uncomplaining acceptance of the soldier's lot has proved another endearing quality to the family. For example, in asking his wife to send him an "ointment," he told her it is "hard to keep clear of vermin."[12] And again, explaining why he kept some of his pay instead of sending it all to Margaret when the regiment was about to go on a forced march, he told her that if a man has a few dollars in his pocket, he can sometimes buy a bit of butter or milk from a farmer. But failing that, he added, "You have no idea how one will relish a dry cracker without anything with it."[13]

And before his only furlough was granted, he warned Margaret that there were others in the company ahead of him; it was only fair that they should go home first. Then he added: "If I can't get home, I must only content myself the best I can until next fall and then please God I will have a furlough."[14]

Thus, for the family, these letters bear witness to the transformation of a simple "foot soldier," as he called himself, to a man of resolute devotion to wife, country, and God, a man who stands tall among the thousands of Irish immigrants in the Civil War. And that man is Peter Welsh, colorbearer and patriot!

THE WIFE MARGARET
AS THE FAMILY REMEMBERS HER

When word reached Margaret that Peter was in Carver Hospital in Washington, she prepared at once to go to him. He had cautioned her not to be "uneasy about me,"[15] but she was frightened. On arrival at the hospital she soon learned that doctors had recommended amputation of the injured arm. She pleaded with her husband to allow this.

At that moment she remembered one special letter in which Peter had assured her that "If it were my misfortune to be disabled or lose an arm or leg, which God forbid, then I would accept it as the will of God."[16] But Peter had put his trust in God. And had not God brought him "out safe" from many battles? Would God not now heal that "flesh wound"?

Whatever his thoughts, and hers, this generation will never know. What is known is that, despite his wife's pleading, Peter would not submit to amputation. He could not at that time agree to a handicap that would prevent him from making a living in the only trade he knew. However, there was surgery to remove the bullet and shattered bone fragments. Blood poisoning in the form of pyemia followed, and Peter died.[17]

Margaret took her husband home. He was buried in an Old Calvary grave that had been purchased by her uncle, James Gleason, in 1855 and was now given over to Margaret in her hour of need. The deed would be formally transferred to her August 22, 1887. After the funeral she devoted herself to the design and erection of Peter's elegant monument.[18]

Meanwhile she applied for a widow's pension, identified as No. 68983, in the amount of eight dollars a month. And on February 23, 1865 she was awarded $342.86 by the United States Treasury

Department as back pay owed to her husband from February to May 28, 1864. This included $110 still due the soldier from the bounty he merited for re-enlisting.

Once the most urgent business matters were settled, she took the first of what would become many trips home to her family in Athy, County Kildare.[19] Her sister Sarah, the next oldest of the seven children of Michael and Mary O'Toole Prendergast, was married in Athy July 6, 1865 to Michael Joseph Hoey of Bagenalstown. The following June their first child, a son James, was born in Athy. Margaret Welsh was in Ireland at this time and had arranged to receive thirteen pounds sterling through the Ulster Bank in Belfast, while still in New York on March 9, 1866.[20]

Soon thereafter the Michael Hoeys settled in New York, and Margaret Welsh made her home with them whenever she was not in Ireland. St. Michael's Church records in Athy certify that she was a sponsor at the baptism June 6, 1875 of Mary, the infant daughter of her brother Patrick and his wife Catherine Lawler Prendergast.

Margaret Welsh did not enjoy robust health. Because of this her effort to supplement her income through domestic service while her husband was in the army had to be abandoned in less than a month. Similarly, she was gifted in sewing, but her husband discouraged her from seeking employment of this kind because he knew she could not tolerate the stress.[21] She did, however, have an appreciation of feminine charm, for a newspaper clipping describing how to make "Fragrant Perfumes and Washes" was tucked into her portfolio along with Peter's letters. As a "refreshing odor for the bath," the article suggested "an ounce of clove pink petals infused in three-quarters of a pint of pure alcohol with a few verbena leaves." The article continued to describe the preparation of emollients as a cooling remedy for sunburn, and concluded that "Some of the beauties of old used to swear by the good effects of a raw potato, cut in half, and rubbed on the face at night."

Because Margaret's health was restrictive, she turned to simple diversions such as crocheting and embroidering. She also enjoyed the activities of the three Hoey children, especially going out with them for walks. When nothing else was happening to require her attention, there was always Polly. The gift of a friend, the parrot was Aunt Marda's special pet. Over the years, Polly developed quite a vocabulary, with the result that a number of anecdotes featuring what Polly said, or did, became a living storybook in the Hoey household.

In June 1879 Marda was admitted to membership in the Confraternity of the Most Holy and Immaculate Heart of Mary, initiated at the church of St. Vincent de Paul in New York, and united with the Arch-Confraternity established in the church of Our Lady of Victories, Paris. This membership required many religious duties, which she embraced wholeheartedly.[22]

Margaret and Peter had no children, and she never married again. Thus her keepsake mementos, together with the ritual of her Church and the love of her family, fostered the spiritual peace and tranquillity that characterized the widowhood of Margaret Prendergast Welsh.

NOTES

1. See illustration.
2. Letter of December 30, 1862.
3. Letter of February 22, 1863.
4. Letter of February 3, 1863.
5. Letter of March 31, 1863.
6. Letter of September 19, 1863.
7. Letter of February 3, 1863.
8. Letter of March 31, 1863.
9. Letter of October 23, 1862.
10. Letter of May 27, 1863.
11. Letter of December 25, 1862.
12. Letter of December 30, 1862.
13. Letter of January 7, 1863.
14. Letter of December 31, 1863.
15. Letter of May 15, 1864.
16. Letter of February 22, 1863.
17. George A. Otis, *The Medical and Surgical History of the War of the Rebellion*, Part II, Vol. 2, *Surgical History* (Washington, D.C.:

Government Printing Office, 1877), p. 959: "Fatal Intermediary Excisions in the Forearm . . . Case 1916—Sergeant P. Welsh, Co. K, 28th Massachusetts."

18. Records of Old Calvary Cemetery, 49-02 Laurel Hill Boulevard, Woodside, New York. See illustrations of the monument.

19. Transatlantic passage from New York to Ireland was advertised in the *Pilot*, July 18, 1863, p. 8 col. 4, at $30, all-inclusive. Advertisements announcing sailings appeared regularly under the heading "Steamships." One, on January 11, 1862, p. 8 col. 2, announced rates for passengers landing or embarking at Queenstown, Ireland, at $75 for first cabin; $30, steerage. Sailing dates could be arranged through John G. Dale, agent, 15 Broadway, New York. Oscar Handlin, *Boston's Immigrants: A Study in Acculturation* (Cambridge: The Belknap Press of Harvard University Press, 1959), claims that "The opening by the Cunard Line of regular transatlantic steam communication in 1842 kept rates so low that even the poor could cross" (p. 48). Citing the *Pilot* of January 12, 1856 and December 4, 1858, he states that "By the fifties, one could travel from Liverpool to Boston on a respectable line such as Enoch Train and Company, Page, Richardson, or Wheeler & Armstrong for from $17 to $20, including provisions . . ." (pp. 49 and 314 *n*105).

20. See illustration.

21. Letter of March 8, 1863.

22. Document of the Confraternity of the Most Holy and Immaculate Heart of Mary, containing extracts from the rules, and certification that on June 15, 1879, Margaret Welsh was admitted to membership, found in her portfolio along with the soldier's letters and military papers.

CHRONOLOGY

1830	June 29	Peter Welsh born in Charlottetown, Prince Edward Island.
1857	Sept. 20	Marries Margaret Prendergast in Charlestown, Massachusetts.
1862	Sept. 3	Enlists in 28th Massachusetts Volunteers in Charlestown, Massachusetts.
	Sept. 13	Joins 28th Massachusetts at Nolan's Ferry on the Potomac River.
	Sept. 14	Battle of South Mountain.
	Sept. 17	Battle of Antietam.
	Oct. 23–Nov. 4	Promoted corporal and made acting quartermaster/commissary sergeant.
	Nov. 23	28th Massachusetts joins the Irish Brigade.
	Dec. 13	Battle of Fredericksburg.
1863	Jan. 20–23	"Mud March" of the Army of the Potomac.
	March 17	St. Patrick's Day celebration in the Irish Brigade; made color sergeant of the 28th Massachusetts.
	April 8	President Lincoln makes Grand Review of the Army of the Potomac.
	May 1–4	Battle of Chancellorsville.
	July 1–3	Battle of Gettysburg.
	July 13–16	Draft riots in New York City.
	Sept. 1	Officially attains rank of sergeant.
	Nov. 26–Dec. 1	Mine Run campaign.
	Dec. 31	Discharged to re-enlist in the 28th Massachusetts.

1864 Jan. 1   Re-enlists in 28th Massachusetts as
                        sergeant.
      Feb. 27–Apr. 2   Home on furlough in New York City.
      May 5–7   Battle of the Wilderness.
      May 8–19   Battle of Spotsylvania.
      May 12   Wounded at Spotsylvania.
      May 28   Dies at Carver Hospital in
                        Washington, D.C.
      June 1   Buried at Calvary Cemetery in
                        Queens County, N.Y.

Introduction

LAWRENCE FREDERICK KOHL

SEVERAL HOURS BEFORE DAWN on December 13, 1862, Corporal Peter Welsh awoke with the rest of the Irish Brigade in Fredericksburg, Virginia. As he shook the heavy frost off his blanket and began to cook his breakfast he could not have known what a terrible fate awaited the brigade on that cold December day. The fog did not begin to lift until mid-morning, but by noon the sun was visible and the brigade was drawn up in line of battle in one of the streets of Fredericksburg, ready to assault at a moment's notice the strong Confederate position on the heights above the town. For nearly three weeks Lee had been massing guns and troops on this ridge. And to reach it, the Irish Brigade would have to cross a broad open plain, exposing themselves to the full force of the Confederates' firepower. One member of the brigade approached Rev. William Corby, chaplain of the 88th New York, and expressed his fear that the men were going to be ordered to make this suicidal assault. But Father Corby told him not to be troubled, because, he said, "your generals know better than that." But they did not.[1]

At 2:00 P.M., after four brigades had already been shattered in their attempt to reach the Confederate lines on Marye's Heights, the Irish Brigade received the order to advance onto the plain. Enemy batteries pounded their lines from three sides. Confederate infantry four-deep fired from behind a stone wall with devastating effect. The storm of shot and shell was "terrible," Peter Welsh wrote his wife afterward, "mowing whole gaps out of our ranks and we having to march over their dead and wounded bodies." The brigade braved the storm as long as it could, but, like the rest, it too was broken by the fearful Con-

1

federate fire. Those men who were not already hit sought cover as best they could, some using their dead comrades to shield them from the hail of gunfire. Only under cover of darkness that night were many able to make their way back to town safely.[2]

The fiasco at Fredericksburg hit the army and the Union cause hard, but the day dealt a nearly mortal blow to the Irish Brigade. When the men were called to arms the morning after the battle, only 280 appeared of the more than 1,200 who had gone into action the day before. When the Irish-American community heard of the slaughter they were dismayed and bitter. The Boston *Pilot*, national organ of the American Irish, found plenty of blame for abolitionists, rebels, the Lincoln administration, and General Burnside to share. When the army suffered still another embarrassing and costly defeat at Chancellorsville in the spring, the *Pilot* announced that "the Irish spirit for the war is dead! Absolutely dead! There are a great many Irish yet. But our fighters are dead. . . . Their desperate valor led them, not to victory, but extinction. . . . How bitter to Ireland has been this rebellion!"[3]

But through it all Peter Welsh did not lose heart. Only six weeks after the crushing defeat at Fredericksburg, he wrote his wife, Margaret, that it was the duty of all to do everything in their power "to sustain for the present and to perpetuate for the benefit [of] future generations a government and a national asylum which is superior to any the world has yet known." He admitted that there were flaws in the edifice and that the war itself had been mismanaged by the corrupt and the incompetent, but despite everything, he concluded, "there is yet something in this land worth fighting for." And he continued to believe this until his death on May 28, 1864 of a wound received at the battle of Spotsylvania.[4]

Of course, Peter Welsh may not have been typical of the nearly 150,000 Irish who fought for the Union. Bell Irvin

Wiley, the best authority on the common soldier of the Civil War, thought the Irish less idealistic than the soldiers of other nationalities. To Wiley, their predominant motivation was "the sheer love of combat."[5] But the Civil War letters of Peter Welsh reveal not only a fighter, but a man with a well-developed notion of what he was fighting for. They present thoughtful, closely-reasoned arguments for Irish-American support of the Union cause. Newspapers like the New York *Herald* and the Boston *Pilot* may have helped him to formulate his ideas; nonetheless, he held these ideas deeply, and they justified and gave meaning to the sacrifices Welsh made for his adopted country. They remind us not to be too quick to generalize about our more common ancestors. Perhaps if we could know them all the way these letters allow us to know Peter Welsh, we might find them a more complex and interesting people than we had believed.

Although his thoughtful nature may have set him apart, in many other ways Welsh was typical of the Irish Catholics who fought in the Union army. A handsome man, Welsh was five feet eight-and-a-half inches tall, had hazel eyes and brown hair. He was born in Charlottetown, Prince Edward Island on June 29, 1830. Beyond this, little is known of his early life. Sometime between 1830 and 1857 Peter and one or more of his siblings came to the United States and settled in the Boston area. In the latter year Peter married Margaret Prendergast, who was born in Ireland, one of seven children of Patrick and Margaret O'Toole Prendergast of Athy in County Kildare. The ceremony was performed by the Rev. Aloysius Janalick in St. Mary's Church at the corner of Winthrop and Warren Streets in Charlestown, Massachusetts.[6]

Shortly after their marriage, Margaret and Peter moved to New York City where Peter sought work as a carpenter. But their life together in these years must have been difficult. Peter's war-time letters allude to problems in finding work, bouts of

heavy drinking, and the many "days, weeks, and months of unhappiness" he had brought his wife. More problems with his
own family eventually led to his enlistment in the army. In the
summer of 1862, Peter traveled back to Boston, evidently to try
to resolve some differences between members of his family living there. But instead of becoming the peacemaker, he got
caught in the middle and became the target of both sides in the
dispute. Despondent at this development, he turned to the bottle, went on a "spree," and spent every cent he had brought
with him. When sobriety returned, he was so ashamed of his
behavior that he could not face anyone he knew. Enlistment
as a private in Co. K of the 28th Massachusetts Volunteer Infantry, then recruiting in Charlestown, provided him with a way
out. It would not be an easy way out, however.[7]

The Gaelic motto of the 28th Massachusetts was "Fag-an-
bealac," or "clear the road," and it suited them well, for this
was a fighting regiment. Few regiments saw more action in the
Civil War than the 28th Massachusetts, and few paid a higher
price in casualties. When Welsh joined the regiment they had
already seen action at James Island in South Carolina and at
Second Bull Run and Chantilly in Virginia. In the twenty
months he spent with the 28th, Peter Welsh fought at South
Mountain, Antietam, Fredericksburg, Chancellorsville, Gettysburg, the Wilderness, and Spotsylvania. And though Peter
Welsh, along with so many others, fell from the ranks, the regiment continued to fight on. In the closing days of the war, even
after Cold Harbor, Petersburg, Deep Bottom, and Hatcher's
Run had taken their toll, a remnant of the 28th remained to
pursue Lee's army all the way to Appomattox Court House.
The distinguished record of the 28th Massachusetts on such
celebrated battlefields deserves a wider reputation. Of the
more than 2,000 regiments raised by the North during the
war, only six suffered a larger number of killed and mortally

wounded. The regiment's total casualties for the war totaled 1,199, far more than ever served in it at any one time.[8]

Welsh's letters to his wife, Margaret, began on September 14, 1862, only a day after he had joined the regiment and a day on which the 28th had been engaged at the battle of South Mountain. They ended with his letter of May 15, 1864 from Carver Hospital in Washington, where he had been taken after being wounded at Spotsylvania. In his sixty-five letters that survive from this period[9] he comments on the usual concerns of the common soldier: camp life, long marches, descriptions of battle, attitudes toward officers, and the conduct of the war. But he also provides fascinating insights into his views on blacks, the causes of the war, the justification of the rebellion, his own reasons for supporting the Union, the views of the Catholic Church on war, British involvement in the war, the New York draft riots of 1863, the history of Irish oppression, and what America means to the Irish.

Though the collection is not large, and, of course, not all letters discuss important topics, Welsh's letters are valuable for providing an articulate, immigrant Irish-Catholic perspective on the Civil War. They are all the more remarkable for coming from a common soldier. In addition, they are the first significant collection of letters by a soldier in the Irish Brigade to be published, the first contemporary account of any kind by an enlisted man in the brigade to be published, and the first contemporary account by anyone in the 28th Massachusetts to be published.

It is one of the sad ironies of history that Welsh's misfortunes led to our benefit. Had he not been separated from his wife by war, he probably never would have put pen to paper to record his thoughts for us to read. And had he survived the war, Margaret would have had less reason to preserve so carefully these mementos of a beloved husband. And finally, had Margaret and her family supported Peter in his devotion to the Union, he would never have written the long letters of justification which are so revealing and interesting to us today.

But Margaret did not feel as Peter did about the war, and he was forced to risk his life knowing that those closest to him did not support his efforts. Margaret lamented the fact that he had joined the army and wanted him to resign if he ever got the chance. She dismissed his allusions to St. Paul and Archbishop Hughes to justify the Union cause. She even complained when he wrote her on stationery that bore patriotic slogans. Peter also felt the need to explain his enlistment to Margaret's father, Patrick Prendergast, because, as he said, "I know pretty well in what light people view soldiering in Ireland." He admitted that his actions must seem "unaccountable," but, in a long letter of June 1, 1863, he attempted to explain himself by noting "a few of the many powerful motives that influence Irishmen to take up arms in defense of this government."[10]

Peter Welsh must have been aware, as many of the American Irish were, that the majority sentiment in Ireland was against northern prosecution of the war. There were many reasons for pro-southern sympathies in Ireland. Some nationalists saw a parallel between the southern cause and their own struggle for independence from Britain. Irish Tories, like their British counterparts, were anxious for the break-up of the republican competitor to British supremacy in the world. Some Liberals based their support of the South on abstract principles of self-determination, while others were merely concerned with the diplomatic self-interest of Britain. Finally, there were those Irish, particularly after Fredericksburg, who objected to the further prosecution of the war simply because it was spilling too much Irish blood. Those American Irish, like Peter Welsh, who had dedicated themselves to the Union cause, sometimes became annoyed at criticism from those in the old country.

Welsh, respectful of his father-in-law, chose to write him an eloquent defense of his own position. But others agreed with the Boston *Pilot* when it gave such critics the testy reply: "Let our Irish contemporaries have nothing to do with matters they do not comprehend."[11]

Lack of support for his devotion to the Union was not the only burden Peter Welsh carried on his long marches and bore into battle. The poor health and unhappiness of his wife must have weighed heavily on him. Margaret's health seems never to have been very good, and few of Peter's letters were without a reference to her latest complaint and a wish from Peter that God would soon relieve her suffering. Her physical problems may well have been a consequence of her nervous temperament. Margaret's days were filled with anxious worry. Peter himself made the connection in his letter of April 10, 1863, when he told her that if she wished to improve her health she must try to keep her spirits up and not be "fretting and worrying" the way she had been. His admonitions were of no avail, however, for she wrote him three months later that "I have no heart, no courage, or no strength. I am nearly broken hearted. . . . This is a world of trials and misery." One can well imagine the toll such words must have taken on Peter, a man who loved his wife dearly.[12]

Despite this lack of support, Peter Welsh managed to keep his spirits up throughout his service with the 28th. One reason for his buoyant nature was that army life agreed with him. The conditions that disturbed so many soldiers—the food, long marches, the pay—did not seem to bother him. To Welsh, the food was "plain and strong, but a good appetite makes it very sweet." He confessed later that he had gained fifteen pounds since he entered the service. He also spoke appreciatively of the fresh air and exercise he got in the army and credited it with the good health he had enjoyed since enlisting. He took pride in reporting that while others often fell out of the ranks on hard marches, he always led the way into camp. Even army pay, as meager and irregular as it was, elicited some approving words. Peter wrote Margaret that had he remained at home he would certainly have had "hard times to contend with." Before he enlisted, he reminded his wife, "it was really heart-sickening to be trying to get along at carpenter work the way times were."[13]

Welsh also found more support for his view of the war in the army, especially after the 28th Massachusetts joined the Irish Brigade in the fall of 1862 a few weeks before the battle of Fredericksburg. The Irish Brigade, originally consisting of the 63rd, 69th, and 88th New York infantry regiments, was raised in the fall of 1861 by Thomas Francis Meagher. The creation of an all-Irish brigade to fight for the Union met with some enthusiasm at this time despite the fact that Irish-Americans at first appeared unlikely materials out of which to build a force to subdue the South.

The Irish were staunch Democrats, and many of their chief spokesmen had expressed pro-southern opinions during the sectional controversies that filled the antebellum years. There was also little sympathy for the slave among a people who saw black liberation as a threat to their own position in American society. Economic competition, in particular, between the Irish and free blacks in New York laid the foundation for the draft riots that would tear the city apart in 1863. Nor had the Irish forgotten the nativist antipathy toward them that had flourished only a few years before the war. Though it was not so virulent in 1861, the Irish knew that it was not dead, but sleeping in the membership of the Republican Party which now led them off to war on the South.

Life had not been easy for the hundreds of thousands of Irish who had come to America since the Great Famine. Trapped by poverty in the alien environment of the eastern seaboard's largest cities, they found themselves residentially segregated, condemned to the lowest rungs of the economic ladder, and socially outcast. They practiced their Catholicism in an over-whelmingly Protestant country and enjoyed their whiskey in an era when the temperance movement was winning striking legislative victories. Had they not rallied to the defense of their adopted country and enthusiastically answered the call to arms of a Republican President, no one should have been surprised.

But many did answer the call, particularly when it came from one of their own, like Thomas Francis Meagher. Irish-born and Jesuit-educated, Meagher was the son of a wealthy merchant and member of Parliament. Through his oratorical genius he had become a leader of the Young Ireland party; but the same genius had also gotten him banished to Tasmania for a seditious speech made during the abortive Rising of '48. After a daring escape from the prison colony in Tasmania, Meagher sailed to New York where he became an instant ce-lebrity. Taking out citizenship papers, he lectured, edited the *Irish News*, practiced law, and married Elizabeth Townsend, daughter of a wealthy New York merchant. When the war broke out he was one of the acknowledged leaders of the Ameri-can Irish community.[14]

He had also been known as a man with southern sympathies. But when Fort Sumter was fired upon, he hurried to raise a company of Irish Zouaves to fight with the 69th New York State Militia led by Michael Corcoran. When Corcoran was captured by the Confederates at First Bull Run, it was left to Meagher to create an all-Irish brigade for the Union army. Although the brigade was designed to have regiments raised in New York, Boston, and Philadelphia, only the New York regiments left for the front in the fall of 1861. It was not until nearly a year later that Peter Welsh's regiment, which had been raised specifically for the brigade, actually joined it. A Phila-

9

delphia regiment, the 116th Pennsylvania, also joined the brigade in the fall of 1862, finally giving it the organization that Meagher had contemplated the previous year.[15]

Within the brigade Peter Welsh found sustenance for his view of the war. There fellow Irishmen, led by Irishmen, accompanied by Catholic chaplains, could strike a blow for their adopted country and prove themselves worthy of full citizenship. Their exploits were chronicled in the Irish-American newspapers, most notably in the Boston *Pilot*, which on September 27, 1862, instituted a series entitled "Records of Irish-American Patriotism." The object of the series "was to demonstrate that although the Celts might be hyphenated Americans in name, they were one hundred percent Americans in deed." According to Peter Welsh, "Here Irishmen and their descendants have a claim, a stake in the nation, and an interest in its prosperity." A foreign-born citizen who held himself aloof from the struggle would be "false to his own and his fellow citizen's interests."[16]

Moreover, a victory for the Union would also be a victory for Ireland on two fronts. It would preserve an asylum for Erin's oppressed, and, at the same time, it would strike a blow at Ireland's oppressor. As Welsh argued, "England hates this country because of its growing power and greatness." America's navy and commerce had already surpassed England's, and, with only a few more years of peaceful progress, this country could surpass England "as a manufacturing nation, and England's star of ascendancy will have set to rise no more."[17]

But Welsh contemplated more direct attacks on England too. He claimed to have hoped since childhood "that I might one day have an opportunity, when the right man to lead should be found and the proper time should arrive, to strike a blow for the rights and liberty of Ireland." He considered the American Civil War as "a school of instruction for Irishmen" for such an opportunity. And, "if the day should arrive within ten years after this war is ended, an army can be raised in this country that will strike terror to the Saxon's heart." There were others in the brigade with similar thoughts, General Meagher among them. And not all of them were members of the Fenian brotherhood, that secret revolutionary society organized in Ireland and the United States to achieve Irish independence from England by force. Meagher himself did not join the Fenians until after he had resigned his commission and left the brigade.[18]

Welsh's purposes, then, like the brigade's, were both American and Irish. And it was fitting that the regiments of the brigade went into battle bearing both the stars and stripes and green banners emblazoned with an Irish harp. The proudest day of Welsh's young life was the day he was selected to carry the green flag for the 28th Massachusetts. During the brigade's famous St. Patrick's Day festivities, on March 17, 1863, Welsh was made color sergeant of the regiment. He told Margaret that he felt "proud to bear up that flag of green, the emblem of Ireland and Irish men, and especially having received it on that day dear to every Irish heart." He vowed in a letter to his father-in-law that "it shall never kiss the dust while I have strength to hold it."[19] And through Chancellorsville, Gettysburg, and the Wilderness it never did. But on May 12, 1864, at Spotsylvania Court House, a Confederate bullet shattered the arm that held the flag, and it was left to another Irishman to pick up the green banner. Carried to the rear, Welsh never rejoined his regiment. He died two weeks later at Carver Hospital in Washington.

NOTES

1. Letter of December 25, 1862; Catton, *Army of the Potomac*, II 49–50; William Corby, c.s.c., *Memoirs of Chaplain Life* (Notre Dame: Scholastic Press, 1894), p. 131.

2. Letter of December 25, 1862; Catton, *Army of the Potomac*, II 51–61.

3. *OR*, ser. I, vol. 21, p. 244; Boston *Pilot*, February 14 and May 30, 1863.

4. Letter of February 3, 1863.

5. Wiley, *Billy Yank*, pp. 308–309.

6. Peter Welsh Pension File, NA.

7. Letters of October 11, 1862; October 19, 1862; and February 3, 1863.

8. Fox, *Regimental Losses*, pp. 3, 169; *Mass. Adj.-Gen.* (1865) p. 709, (1866) p. 395.

9. Peter Welsh's letters of December 18 and December 31, 1863 refer to a sixty-sixth letter written to Margaret on December 3, 1863, but this letter cannot be found.

10. Letters of February 8, 1863; February 22, 1863; letter to Patrick Prendergast, June 1, 1863.

11. Hernon, *Celts*, pp. 108, 117–18, 106.

12. Letter of April 10, 1863; Margaret to Peter Welsh, July 12, 1863 (unpublished).

13. Letters of October 11, 1862, February 8, 1863, September 14, 1862, and July 17, 1863.

14. *DAB*.

15. J. L. Garland, "The Formation of Meagher's Irish Brigade," *Irish Sword* 3 (Summer 1958), 162–65, 205.

16. Francis R. Walsh, "The Boston *Pilot* Reports the Civil War," *Historical Journal of Massachusetts* 9 (June 1981), 9; letter to Patrick Prendergast of June 1, 1863.

17. Letter to Patrick Prendergast of June 1, 1863.

18. Ibid.; Athearn, *Meagher*, p. 131.

19. Letter of March 19, 1863; letter to Patrick Prendergast of June 1, 1863. The 28th Massachusetts carried at least three green flags during the war. The first and most elaborate was depicted in a woodcut in the *Pilot* on January 18, 1862. The second, mentioned in the letter of February 16, 1863, was brought out to the regiment by Capt. Charles H. Sanborn on his return from medical leave at Boston. The third was presented to Col. Richard Byrnes at the Parker House in Boston on April 5, 1864, but Byrnes did not rejoin the regiment until six weeks later, and thus brought the flag out to the 28th only after Peter Welsh had been wounded at Spotsylvania. Conyngham, *Irish Brigade*, pp. 442–44. Remnants of two of these flags are preserved in the Massachusetts State House, Boston. See illustrations.

THE
LETTERS

1862

"WE ADVANCED BOLDLY
DESPITE IT ALL"

WHEN PETER WELSH ENLISTED in the 28th Massachusetts on September 3rd, there were only a few months left in 1862. But for Welsh and the 28th, these months would begin and end with action.

Less than a week after enlisting he arrived in camp outside Washington only to find his regiment gone. For Lee's Army of Northern Virginia had crossed the Potomac into Maryland, throwing the North into a panic and causing McClellan's army to leave Virginia in pursuit. After several days of hard marching, Welsh finally caught up with his regiment near Frederick, Maryland, just in time to take part in a sharp fight at South Mountain. Only three days later and just two weeks to the day after his enlistment in the 28th, Welsh helped to turn back Lee at the battle of Antietam.

After that things settled down a bit and he was able to write Margaret long letters about his life in the army. By mid-October he reported that "we have fine easy times now," nothing to do but "eat, sleep, and grow fat." In late November the 28th Massachusetts became part of the famous Irish Brigade, joining them at Falmouth, across the Rappahannock from Fredericksburg, Virginia. There Peter Welsh, like the rest of the army, threw himself into erecting winter quarters. But the year's fighting was not over.

Burnside had replaced McClellan as commander of the Army of the Potomac and the country wanted action. So on December 13th, despite objections from wiser heads, Burnside drove his army against Lee's heavily fortified position across the river. The resulting carnage was terrible and the disaster brought despair to the North. But though there was much stupidity displayed at Fredericksburg, there was also much courage. The Irish Brigade's assault on Marye's Heights was a conspicuous example of that courage. Though the brigade knew the assault was doomed from the start, though they had seen the brigades which had preceded them destroyed, though they had to brave shot and shell, grape and canister, minié and spherical balls to reach a formidable enemy protected by stone walls and fortifications, still they went forward when the word came to advance. For many it would be a march "from earth to eternity." But, Peter Welsh proudly wrote his wife afterward, "We advanced boldly despite it all."

Sunday sept the 14th/62

My dear dear wife

i take the first oppertunity of writing to you   i am now between fredricks citty and harpers ferry   i would wrote before but i did not reach the regment untill yesterday and then we had to start on a march again   we got allog quite easy untill we reached washington but since that we had to march   we were sent to join our regment about eight miles out of washington but when we got there they were gone and we had to march from tuesday evening to saturday morning before we cot them   My dear wife I am in good health thank God   there is not a man that left with me can stand it better so far   there is a great many that started with me behind on the road   they were not able to keep up   now my dear wife do not fret nor be uneasy about me   the only thing that frets me is being away from you   it grieves my heart to think that you are there so lonly but keep up your spirits   i will soon be back with you pleas God   you know i never would have left you only i was crazy from that acursed missfortune i fell intoo   however you need not be afraid of my drinking now for there is no licker alowed in the army nor no person is alowed to sell it to soldiers and that is much the best   there is hundreds of men here who got in to it in the same way as i did   but do not think that i am sory for coming for it was my wish [to] come   the only thing i am sory for is leaving you allone and for the unfortunate spree drove me to it   About the relief mony[1] i understand it can be drawn at any time so that if i am long out here which i dont expect to be you could go on and draw it any time before i got back   My dear wife you must try and make yourself as comfortable as you can   and keep our furniture if you possibly can if you can get any place to keep them for there is no knowing how soon i may be home   we new recruits will have no fiting to do for some time untill we are drilled and armed our army are after stonewall jackson[2]   they took over three thousand rebel prisoners yesterday[3]   now my dear wife i must conclud with the fervent wish that God may bless and protect you untill i see you again   you may expect another letter from me soon if i have an oppertunity to write   Adress your letter to

Peter Welsh 28th Regt Mass V
Company K Washington D C
fare well for the present my dear and loving wife   may angels
guard you   write to me ass soon as possible   adue

your loving husband
PETER WELSH

1. Margaret Welsh was entitled to receive a monthly stipend under the provisions of Chap. 222 of the *Acts and Resolves Passed by the General Court of Massachusetts in the Year 1861* (Boston: White, 1861), "An Act in Aid of the Families of Volunteers, and for Other Purposes." Section 1 of that act enabled Massachusetts towns and cities to raise money for the aid of the wives, children, or other dependents of men who were "mustered into or enlisted in the service of the United States." Section 5 provided that, within limits, towns' and cities' expenditures would be reimbursed annually from the state treasury.

2. Thomas Jonathan Jackson (1824–1863) was an 1846 graduate of West Point. Jackson got his sobriquet of "Stonewall" when his brigade stood firm against a Federal onslaught at the first battle of Bull Run. At the time of this letter General Jackson was probably the most famous Confederate commander. His Shenandoah Valley campaign against far superior Union forces in the spring of 1862 had made him a southern hero and Lee's most trusted lieutenant. On September 14 he was making his final preparations for the capture of Harper's Ferry. The next day 11,500 Union soldiers at the Ferry surrendered to him. Jackson died on May 10, 1863 shortly after the battle of Chancellorsville in which he had been mistakenly shot by his own troops while making a twilight reconnaissance. *DAB*.

3. There were no significant engagements on the 13th to which Welsh might be referring. Even if this is a reference to the battle of South Mountain fought on September 14th, the number of rebel prisoners taken is almost certainly too high. The most authoritative estimate puts the number of prisoners taken by the Army of the Potomac on this date at 1800. Livermore, *Numbers & Losses*, p. 94.

Camp near harpers ferry   Sept 21st

Dear wife

i wrote you a letter last sunday which I hope you have got before this   i told you in it that i had no chance to write sooner as i did not reach my regment untill the day before i mentioned in it   but for fear you might not get it i will repeat it that wish you would keep the furniture if you possibly can for i may be home sooner then you expect   i know it is hard for you to manage situated as you are but there is no help for it now   you must do the best you can and with Gods blessing all will be right before long   i will not write much this time as i am anxious to hear from you and then i will write you a long letter   be of good cheer dear wife and may God bless and protect you and take me back safe to you once more

your loving husband
PETER WELSH

direct your letter to

Peter Welsh Company K
28th Regment Mass Vol
Washington D C

Camp of pleasent Valy   October 11th/62

My dear wife

i received your long looked for letter last night   it was a source
of great conselation to me for i was very uneasy that i did not have
a letter from you before   i was afraid that you were sick and did
not wish to let me know   but thank God it is not so   yesterday was
my turn on guard and when i came into camp to get my supper
the letters were giving out   i cannot describe the satisfaction it
gave me when i opened the letter and found it was from your self
my dear wife you must not worry and fret so   your case is not any
worse then thousands of others   and one consalation you will have
plenty of means to support you and not go to kill yourself slaving
and working for the miserable price you would get for it   i can
send you my pay as soon as i get it   and if i had remained at home
i feel sertain we would had hard times to contend with   another
thing i feel confident of that this war must be ended very soon   and
even though i should have to serve a year which i hope i wont nor
more then half but even at a year i would be better paid then working at my trade supposing i got constant work which i could not
those times and then should beg for what i would get   it was realy
heartsickning to be trynd to get along at carpenter work the way
times were   As for going home i am heartily sorry for ever thinking
of it   i know i would never be contented there and what was worse
i know you would have a still wors time then me placed as you
would be between two conflicting parties   it is most certain that
both would be disatisfied with you and with each other and you
could have but little happiness in such a position   the fact is that
with both you and me in that case our good nature overcame our
reason or we would have seen it in a different light   i wish it was
settled for mothers sake but i believe it was not to be by my going
there   as for joining the army i have but two causes for regret
the greatest of which is having to be seperated from you and the
other is that i went to Boston atall   i would much rather i had come
in a New York regment   As for your fretting and worying about
me it is folly if you look at it in the right light   i am in good health
thank God and never was so hearty in my life   i believe i can eat
more here in one day then i would in two at home   exercise in the

open air agrees with me better then anything else our food of course is plain and strong but a good apetite makes it very sweet we do not allways get all or what we ought to get espesialy when we are marching but there is allways plenty to eat when we are in camp so that the provisions can come up there is some cases of cource where through the fault of the quartermaster rations cannot be had when due but that is not often so far as i have seen but they have to come to the mark if they are properly looked after About sending anything to me it would not be any use untill i write to you to send them as i do not know how long we will be here yet but if we go into quarters there is a few things i will want you to send me i think it is most likely we will be stationed here or at harpers ferry which is about four miles distant we have been in camp for the last three weeks expt one march of about ten miles There is one thing i am very sory for that our chaplin is not with us he went home sick but we expect him or another in his place here very soon the chaplin that was with the regment was father McMahon[1] I did not get a certificate for the relief yet[2] i was waiting to hear from you if i can get it to day i will send it in this letter if not i will send it in my next which i will write you in a few days about your going to Boston i would not wish you to go to live there upon any account for i know you would not feel contented nor happy there now and espesialy as your uncle and ant have went to live to New York[3] you can board with them and feel at home and be much more comfortable i am very glad they are there and that you had the place for them to stop in if the relief mony can not be drawn for you by anyone in boston i have been told that it can be let lay and drawn at any time that you would go after it i can not write any more in this so i must conclude untill my next

Your affectionate husband
PETER WELSH

1. Rev. Laurence McMahon was mustered in as chaplain of the 28th Massachusetts on June 28, 1862 at Boston. He resigned and was honorably discharged on May 30, 1863 due to a disability incurred in the line of duty. Germain, *Catholic Chaplains*, p. 84.

2. "General Order No. 27 of the Adjutant-General, Commonwealth of Massachusetts," required "certificates on enlistment" to be issued "to parties applying to the municipalities for aid under the State Soldiers Families' Relief Law." Without this certificate as proof of enlistment, aid under the relief law as well as any future bounties or pensions might be withheld. Mass. War Records.

3. Margaret Welsh lived with her uncle James Gleason and his wife at 28 Madison St. in New York City while Peter served in the army.

[mid-October 1862][1]

My dear wife

i have written three letters to you since i came out and received but one   the last one i sent on the 14th   i sent you $60 dollars at the same time   i seen James Byrnes[2]   he told me you had a bad tooth acke   i hope you got well of it before this   i am in excelant health thank god   I wrote a letter to Ellen[3] since I wrote to you you can put an envelope on this letter and sent it to Irland   good by for the present   god be with you

your loving husband
PETER WELSH

1. This letter bears no date, but internal evidence places it between the 14th and the 19th of October, 1862.

2. James E. Byrnes was a close friend of Margaret and Peter Welsh. He was 23 years old when he was mustered in as a private in the 88th New York Volunteers in December of 1861. Byrnes rose through the ranks to first lieutenant before he was killed in action at the Battle of Cold Harbor, June 3, 1864. Phisterer, *New York in the War*, IV 2983.

3. This is probably Ellen Welsh, sister of Peter. In 1857 she had been in Boston to witness her brother's wedding, but she was evidently in Ireland at the time this letter was written.

Camp in pleasant Vally   Oct the 19th/62

My dear wife

i received your kind letter of the 13th last night   i got your first letter on the 10th and wrote you a letter the next day   i sent you a certificate in it to draw the state aid   about the back pay you have been missinformed   they have got to pay it from the day i was sworn into the service   i do not know whether you get it drawn and sent to you or not   i cincerly hope you can for i do not wish you to stop in boston   i know you would feel much more lonesome there then where you are   My dear wife do for your own sake and for my sake try and cheer up your spirits and do not fret and worry yourself so much   you make yourself miserable and you make me feel most wreched to know that you are so unhappy i pray God may grant you peace of mind and strenght to bear up under your trials   If you do not go to Boston right away send that eleven dollars to amelia[1]   i do not want her to think that she is going to loose it   the three dollars you sent home they will send back if amelia has wrote home and let them know where i am   i would like you to write to mother and tell her how it was that i did not go home   I was placed in a hard position   if i went home then i would not had mony to pay my way back   if i could not arange matters for to remain i might be delayed two or three weeks and loose my time and get back with the chance of having nothing to do   thinking of this and the probebility of matters not turning out to our satisfaction if i remaind there these things woried me to such pitch that i did not know what to do nor what i was doing and i got completely reckless   I did not see nor hear anything of Ansels[2] in Boston   in fact i seen very few that i knew there   You mentioned in your letter that John Prendergast[3] said he would write to me from Baltimore   let me know if he is stopping there My dear wife i enjoy excelent health thanks be to God   i am hearty and strong   i havent caught the slightest cold since i came out   the only thing that troubled me was a change in my bowls which was brought on by on by [sic] change of food and water that run me down very weak for a few days but i soon got over it   We have a new colnel appointed to our rigment   the former colnel resighned some time since and one of the captains has been acting

as colnel[4] the new colnels name is Byrne[5] he was a Leutenent
in the regular service and i expect we will have what is much
needed that is better order and decipline in the regment it never
had competent nor efeciant oficers thus the rigment is not what
it would be nor what it ought to be our ranks are cut down very
much we can not muster over three hundred men fit for dudy
there is a great many in hospital wounded we are laying here
now as a reserve and i do not think we will have much more
fighing to do the principle part of this army is ahead of us and
all the new rigments coming out go into the advance of our army
we have have [sic] fine easy times here now nothing but camp guard
to do and eat sleep and grow fat the only hard job i felt since i
came out was the last march we made this part of Maryland is all
mountains and valys we only moved a few miles last time but all
the men said it was the hardest piece of road they ever traveled we
have been laying here now two weeks and we may be here for some
time as it is necessary to keep a force here to prevent the rebels from
crossing the potomac again although there is little danger of
that as they paid to dear for their last trip over here[6] my space
runs short so i must conclude give my love to James gleason[7] and
Ann and to your uncle and aunt and James[8] good by and God
bless and protect you

your affectionate husband
PETER WELSH

1. Cannot identify.
2. Cannot identify.
3. Margaret Welsh had an uncle by this name, although one cannot
be sure that he is the John Prendergast to whom Peter is referring.
4. The original commander of the 28th Massachusetts was Col. William Monteith, a New York City builder who received his commission
on November 25, 1861. But Monteith was placed in arrest by order of
Gen. David Hunter on May 20, 1862, and never resumed command of
the regiment. He resigned from the army at Newport News, Va. on
August 12, 1862. At the time Welsh joined the regiment it was being
commanded by Capt. Andrew P. Caraher, a Boston manufacturer when
he received his commission on October 28, 1861. *Mass. Soldiers*, III 190;
Mass. Adj.-Gen. (1863), pp. 300, 302–303.

5. Col. Richard Byrnes had risen from private to first lieutenant in the U.S. Cavalry before he became colonel of the 28th Massachusetts Volunteer Infantry on September 29, 1862. (See illustration.) He was to command the 28th until June 3, 1864 when he was fatally wounded at the battle of Cold Harbor. D. P. Conyngham reported that he was an outstanding commander: "He commanded the respect and esteem of those under him, and to his efforts is mainly due the high reputation for steadiness and discipline which the Twenty-eighth enjoyed." Francis B. Heitman, *Historical Register and Dictionary of the United States Army*, 2 vols. (Washington, D.C.: Government Printing Office, 1903), I 272; Conyngham, *Irish Brigade*, p. 586. Welsh did not retain his enthusiasm for the leadership of Col. Byrnes, however. See letters of May 13, 1863 and April 14, 1864.

6. The Confederates "last trip over here" was the recently completed Maryland campaign which culminated in the battle of Antietam on September 17th. Both sides "paid too dear" on that day, the bloodiest in American history. Total casualties were 26,134. Livermore, *Numbers & Losses*, pp. 92–93.

7. James and Ann Gleason, son and daughter-in-law of the elder Gleasons, uncle and aunt with whom Margaret Welsh lived during her husband's army service.

8. Cannot identify.

Pleasent Vally   Oct the 23d/62

My dear wife

i received your welcome letter of the 19th to day   it gives me great happiness to receive a letter from you   each letter forms a new epoch in the otherwise dull and disenteresting life of laying idle in camp   the regment are all away about ten miles down the potomac river except our company   this brigade is on picket duty there   our company were detailed here before the rest of the regment went to do guard duty on the camp of another brigade and on private property   but the other brigade came back a week ago and we were relieved from that duty so we have nothing to do now but guard our own camp   this however will not last long as the rigment will come back very soon or elce we will go to them   our new colnel is with them and if they do come back to stay longer here our time will be well taken up with drill   as he belongs to the regular service he will no doubt put us under more strict decipline a thing that is much needed here   we have some very good men and good soldiers and some as miserable specimens of humanity as ever the world produced   this rigment never had oficers competent to make it an efective military body   i hope we will have a change for the better now   there is a good many regiments who have had the same cause of complaint   I was both surprised and disapointed when i joined the regiment to find it what it is   but i se there is one thing certain that irishmen as a generel rule are good soldiers but they must have oficers who are strict military men   but they are not all material to make good soldiers of   there is a good many of them hangers back when fighting is to be done   there is some irishmen as well as of other nations who believe a living coward is better then a dead heroe   I firmly believe that if all the federal army both oficers and men would doe their duty fully and bravely this war would been ended before now   the most fault is with the oficers   in some cases their unfitness for the position they hold and in others the neglect to do their duty while in others their illtreatment of the men under them make the men hate to do anything except what they are forced to do   it is no uncomon thing to hear men swear they will never fire another shot if they can help it and the longer the war lasts the

27

more we are likely to have of this disafected class   however with
the force that is now being pushed forward the war may be ended
without mising the skedadlers or disafected   We had a funeral here
yesterday   a poor fellow by the name of andrew Oneil[1] of Boston
died in our hospital   he had been sick for some time   i made the
poor fellows coffin and had to make it of pieces of old boxes   it is
few here get as good   My dear wife you say you believe my coming
here was to be and from the way you write one would infer that
you think i intended to come when i left new york for boston   but
if you think so you are under a mistake for i had no such intention
then   if i had i would have come in a new york regiment   but that
something would have turnd up to bring me here i believe to be
certain   but thank God i have been very lucky so far   i escaped
all harm in the late battles[2] and enjoy good health   one of the new
recruits that came out when i did got killed at the battle of Antetam
and another who was my camp mate lost his right arm   he was sent
to hospital and i have not heard from him since   he was a very nice
man and has a wife and famely   he was not with me when you seen
me in new york   i have been lucky in getting another camp mate
who is a clean and well conducted man   My dear wife i want you to
send me a sheat of paper and an envelope in the pilot[3]   they are
double price here and i can not cary paper with me without getting
it smashed up

your loving and affectionate husband
PETER WELSH

1. Andrew O'Neal, a private in Co. I of the 28th, died of disease in
October 1862. When he enlisted in October of 1861, O'Neal was a 30-
year-old laborer from Boston. *Mass. Soldiers* III 257.

2. The battles of South Mountain (September 14) and Antietam
(September 17).

3. The Boston *Pilot* was "the most widely read Irish-American newspaper of the nineteenth century." Founded in 1836 by Patrick Donahoe,
it was known as the "Irishman's Bible." The *Pilot* was the successor to
a paper called the *Jesuit*, which Bishop Benedict Fenwick established in
1829 as the voice of the Catholic Church in New England. It was re-
titled twice before its dwindling circulation caused it to be transferred

to Donahoe in 1835. It assumed the name of the *Pilot* in 1836 and was operated as an independent Irish-American weekly until it was sold to the Archdiocese of Boston in 1908. Francis R. Walsh, "The Boston *Pilot* Reports the Civil War," *Historical Journal of Massachusetts* 9 (June 1981), 5, 14.

Camp near Unionvill[1]   November 4th/62

My dear wife

i take this oppertunity to write a few lines to you   i have not received any letter from you since the one you wrote on 18th of October   i wrote you a letter on the 23d and i wrote one a few days before that   you had not got it when you wrote   i got the herald[2] and one pilot that you sent me   we moved from where we were when i wrote last the next day and we crossed the potamac river on last wensday   so we are now in old Virginea   i have not time to write much no as we got to get ready for inspection   we got here late last night   we have only marched three days since we crossed the river but i expect we will have a goodeal of marching to do now as the enemy is retreating   so you must not be uneasy if you do not hear from me regular as i may not have a chance to write I have got the first step towards promotion   i am a corperal and acting quartermasters sergeant for my company   i draw all the rations for the company and serve them out   by having this birth i am exempt from all guard dutty which is some advantage especialy in stormy weather   my dear wife i hope you are well and in good spirits   i am in good health thank God   i can eat everything that comes before me   i must cut this short   i will write you a long letter as soon as i have time

your loving husband
PETER WELSH

---

1. *Mass. Adj.-Gen.* (1863), p. 303, reports that the 28th Massachusetts was camped at Upperville, Virginia on this date. However, Peter Welsh may have been referring to the town of Union, which was in the immediate vicinity.

2. Almost certainly James Gordon Bennett's New York *Herald*. During the war the *Herald* had the largest circulation of any paper in the United States. Although it was politically independent, the *Herald* frequently denounced the Lincoln administration and opposed emancipation of the slaves. Before the war, Bennett had bragged that his was the only northern paper "that has unfailingly vindicated the constitutional rights of the South." Yet the paper remained loyal and, at the last minute, even endorsed Lincoln in the election of 1864. Edwin

Emery, *The Press and America: An Interpretive History of Journalism,* 2nd ed. (Englewood Cliffs, N.J.: Prentice-Hall, 1962), pp. 280, 290–91; Frank Luther Mott, *American Journalism, A History: 1690–1960,* 3rd ed. (New York: Macmillan, 1962), pp. 348–50.

Camp before Fredericksburg   November the 23/62

Dear wife

i feel very uneasy at not hearing from you   the last letter i got from you was wrote on the 18th of October   i got one pilot since but that is all   i have written three letters to you since   i would have written oftener but i did not have time as we have been marching nearly all the time   we arived here on thursday evening after making four forced marches   the last day it was raining and the roads were bad which mad marching purty hard   the weather has been very wet and disagreeable since we came here untill to-day   but i am well and hearty thank God   i seem to grow heartier every day   I expected to have some mony to send you before this but our division have received no pay since i came out   i expect we will get paid very soon   the 69th New York are camped about two miles from us   we passed by there camp coming   i will try to get to see James Burns[1] if I can before i write again   My dear wife i intend [to] give you a full discription of my travels and camp life but i can not mak up my mind to write a long letter untill i hear from you and know how you are getting along   If you put the number of our core and division on the direction of your letters they may come more regular   i will give you the adress on the back of this letter   I must now conclude this short letter by praying that God may bless and protect you and take me home safe to you once more

Your ever affectionate husband
PETER WELSH

Adress your letter to

Peter Welsh Co K
28th Rigement Mass Vol
1st Division 9th Army Core
Washington D C

1. Although his name is almost invariably misspelled, this is James E. Byrnes; see above, p. 23n2.

Camp near Falmouth   November 30th/62

My dear wife

i feel very uneasy about not getting any letters from you   i have not received any letter from you for over a month allthough i have wrote several letters to you since   i sent one last sunday and just after i posted it we got orders to strike tents and move camp   we are now joined with the Irish brigade[1]   i am glad of the change General Meagher[2] reviewed us on monday morning and welcomed us to the brigade   the 88th New York is camped next to us   i have been to see James Burns twice   i seen him last night   he is well he is second leutenent of his company now   his pay amounts to one hundred and five dollars per month which is quite a nice sum[3] I directed you in my last letter to put the number of our division and brigade on the direction of your letters but as we are now in another division[4] that direction will not do   i will give you the adress on the outside of this letter   My dear wife i canot account for being so long without hearing from you   i would feel more uneasy then i do but that i think your letters may have got misslaid on the way   i trust in God that there is nothing the matter with you   I think from the apearence of things that we are likely to remain here for some time   we have an exelent place for camp water is convenient and it is well sheltered from the cold winds My dear wife i must now conclude with hope of hearing from you very soon and that God may bless and protect you

your affectionate husband

PETER WELSH

Adress your letter to

Peter Welsh Co K
28th Regiment Mass Vol
Irish Brigade 1st Division
2nd Army Core
Washington D C

1. According to William F. Fox, "The Irish Brigade was, probably, the best known of any brigade organization, it having made an unusual reputation for dash and gallantry. The remarkable precision of its

evolutions under fire; its desperate attack on the impregnable wall at Marye's Heights; its never failing promptness on every field; and its long continuous service, made for it a name inseparable from the history of the war." When the 28th Massachusetts and the 116th Pennsylvania joined the 63rd, 69th, and 88th New York in the fall of 1862, the brigade had all the regiments "which properly belonged to it." Fox, *Regimental Losses*, p. 118.

2. Gen. Thomas Francis Meagher (1823–1867) organized the Irish Brigade in the winter of 1861–1862. (See illustration.) He commanded it from February 3, 1862 until May 14, 1863 when he resigned his commission, believing that his command's devastated condition had made it but a "poor vestige and relic of the Irish Brigade." Athearn, *Meagher*, p. 125.

3. Unless Welsh is including bounty payments or some other special compensation in this figure, he is mistaken about James Byrnes' pay. Second lieutenants were entitled to only $45.00 per month at this time. Lord, *They Fought for the Union*, p. 123.

4. On November 23, 1862 the 28th Massachusetts moved from the first division of Ambrose Burnside's Ninth Corps to the first division of Edwin V. Sumner's Second Corps.

Camp Near Falmouth   December the 4th/62

My dear wife

i received your welcome letter day before yesterday   i have not received any letters before since one that was dated October the 18th   i do not know why your letters did not come   your not puting the name of the company on them would not prevent them from coming to the regiment   it woud only delay them in the Ajutants quarters untill they found out who they were for   i have received only one pilot since got that letter   My dear wife i am sory you went to the trouble of going to Boston atall   I understood that the state aid was eight dollars per month but it seems that i was missinformed[1]   I am very sory to hear that your health is so bad   i trust in God that you will be better before you get this   you must try and compose your mind and not to fret and worry yourself about me for i am well and hearty and with the blessing of God i will return safe to you before very long   there is no amediate prospect of any fighting here and i [it] is doutfull if we will have any this winter as the roads will be unfit to move troops on as soon as winter sets in   we are in a good position here   the cars run frome here to near Washington and boats can come up the river to this place so that if we should have to stop here we will have no trouble in getting suplies   There is another advantage we have since we joined this brigade   there is three priests with the brigade[2] so the [that] we have frequent oppertunitys of going to mass and evening prayer   I mentioned in my last letter that i seen James Burns and that he is well   we expect to get paid every day and i will send you some mony   we will get paid up to the first of November   they pay every two months so we will get another pay the first of next month   My dear wife i beseech you to try and make your mind easy about me and not destroy your health by keeping yourself in such a freted state for i am just as safe and well here as if i was at home   the same hand that would protect me there can protect me here   may God bless and protect you

your loving husband

PETER WELSH

35

1. The state treasury was to reimburse the towns and cities one dollar per week for aid given to the wives of Massachusetts soldiers. It appears that the aid voted by local governments did not exceed this amount, so Margaret Welsh was probably entitled to a stipend of four dollars a month. *Acts and Resolves . . . 1861*, Chap. 222, Sect. 5; Charles Phillips Huse, *The Financial History of Boston* (Cambridge: Harvard University Press, 1916), p. 124.

2. At this time the three priests who were with the brigade were the Revs. Thomas Ouellett, s.j. (69th N.Y.), William Corby, c.s.c. (88th N.Y.), and Edward McKee (116th Pa.). Fr. Ouellett (also known in an Anglicized form as Willet) was enrolled as chaplain of the 69th New York on November 10, 1861. He was born in Canada and was 41 years old at the time he joined the regiment. After the battle of Fredericksburg, when the 69th was greatly reduced in numbers, Fr. Ouellett was discharged so that he could enter the hospital service in North Carolina. However, he returned to the 69th later in the war (February 14, 1864) when the regiment was reorganized and augmented by new recruits. Germain, *Catholic Chaplains*, pp. 58, 104–107. Fr. Corby served as chaplain of the 88th New York from December of 1861 to September of 1864. His *Memoirs of Chaplain Life* (Notre Dame: Scholastic Press, 1894) are an important source of information about life in the Irish Brigade. After the war Fr. Corby became president of Notre Dame University. Germain, *Catholic Chaplains*, pp. 64–65. Fr. Edward McKee's service with the 116th Pennsylvania was short. He was mustered in as chaplain on September 24, 1862 and was honorably discharged on December 21, 1862 after he tendered his resignation due to illness. Germain, *Catholic Chaplains*, pp. 83–84; Corby, *Memoirs*, p. 19.

Camp near Falmouth   December the 8th/62[1]

My dear wife

i received your last letter on the 4th   i sent you a letter on that day and got yours in the evening   i sent you a letter four days before that   i have not received any of the letters you sent me since the 18th of October untill the last two and i got both of them last week   i got the hearald you sent me last week but i got only two pilots since you first sent them   you had better not put anything in the pilot when you are sending it as that may be the reason they did not come   My dear wife i am very sorry to hear that your health is so bad   you will destroy your health if you do not try and make your mind easier and not fret and wory so much   you must not pay so much regard to what you read in the newspapers for they do not know much about matters here   their blowing about coming battles is all gammon   not even the Generals themselves can tell when a battle will take place   it all depends on circumstances and there is no probability of our having a battle here at present and it is doutfull if there will be any fighting done at this point atall   We have comenced to build houses here for winter quarters so that looks like stopping here for some time   we have got a very good camp ground which is convenient and we have good sheltr wods around us   We had a light fall of snow here on last Friday it is still on the ground and the weather has been purty cold since but we manage to keep purty comfortable by keeping good fires we build our fire at the end of our tent and the heat comes through the canves and warms the inside   we will be better situated however when we get our houses built   You wished to know if i wanted any mony but i have got enough left of what i brought with me yet   buying tobaco is the worst on me   it is very dear here   Sutlers[2] charge an exorbitant price for everything they have   if we remain here i will get you to send me some tobaco and a few other articals i want   it will be time enough after i get paid   we sighned the pay roll last week for two months pay and we expect every day to get it   Our Captains name is Charles H. Sanborn[3]   he is a very good oficer   he belongs to Boston   he lived in south end   i seen James Burns yesterday   he was over to our camp   he is quite well   I mentioned in my last that there is Chaplins with three of

37

the other regiments in the brigade which is very fortunate for us as we have none with our own regiment   I suppose you would like to hear something about camp life   it is sometimes pretty hard but i get along very well   i have excelent health thank God   i am heartier and stronger then i ever remember to be before   i will be quite handy when i get home   we all cook our own coffe in our company and we serve out our pork and bacon raw except when we have beans to boil with our pork   i youst [used] to get meal when i had a chance and fry flap jacks   you would laugh to see us frying them on a tin plate   and our crackers[:] we sometimes soak them and fry them   they go very well for a change   our coffe is very good and that is a great thing for a good mug of coffe when a man is cold or tired refreshes him greatly   i intended to give you a fair description my experience in camp in this but i have to cut it short now to atend to the house building   i will give you a full acount of it as soon as i get time to write a long letter   give my love to James Gleason and wife your uncle and aunt and James and Ann   I must now conclude by praying God to bless and protect you

your affectionate husband
PETER WELSH

1. The letters of December 8, 25, and 30, 1862 were written on poor quality paper that today is crumbling to pieces. Since it is now impossible to derive an accurate text of these letters from the originals, the editors have relied on a typescript of these letters prepared some years ago when they were in better condition.

2. Sutlers were "civilians officially appointed to sell to the troops provisions not furnished by the government." Although their practices and prices were regulated by an 1862 act of Congress entitled "An Act to Provide for the Appointment of Sutlers in the Volunteer Service, and to Define Their Duties," sutlers' practices were often corrupt and their prices exhorbitant. Welsh's opinion of them was not unusual; Donald P. Spear concluded that "the whole class was regarded with contempt, whatever good qualities individuals may have had." "The Sutler in the Union Army," *Civil War History* 16 (June 1970), 121, 124, 137.

3. Charles H. Sanborn was first lieutenant and adjutant of the regiment when he was commissioned in October 1861. (See illustration.) Before the war he had been a submarine engineer in Boston. He was promoted to Captain of Co. K in April of 1862, was wounded at the battle of Fredericksburg, December 13, 1862, and resigned from the service in June of 1863 over differences with the regimental commander, Col. Richard Byrnes. *Mass. Soldiers*, III 190.

Camp near Falmouth   December the 18th/62

My dear wife

i received your welcome letter on the 15th   i would have written right away but i had no paper nor envelopes with me   we were in fredericksburg then we came back here that night and had to go on picket the next morning   so i had no chance to write to you untill now   you have heard of the battle before this[1]   thank God i came out of it safe   it was a fierce and bloody battle   our brigade got teribly cut up   it is so small now that it is not fit to go into any further action unless it is recruited up   so you need not be uneasy now about me for the rest of the fighting will have to be done without our aid   James burns came out safe allso   he is well My dear wife i have not time now to write any more as we are busy fixing up our houses   will write you a long letter in a day or two so i conclud now by wishing Gods blessings be with you

your affectionate husband
PETER WELSH

give my love to all our friends

1. The battle of Fredericksburg, December 13, 1862.

Camp near Falmouth   December the 25th/62

My dear wife

i received your last letter on the 15th   i could not answer i [it] right away as we were then laying in the citty of fredericksburg and i had no means there of writing   and the next morning we had to go on picket so i did not have a chance untill we came back from picket   i then wrote a few lines to you to let you know that i was safe and well thank God   I did not have time to write to you since as we have been as busy as we could be since finishing our houses for winter quarters   i am not quite fixed up yet as i and the Orderly sergeant sleep together and we are fixing a part of the cook house for ourselves   we will have a snug place when it is done   My dear wife it looked very different where i was at mass this morning from where i was this time a year agone   the 88th have an enclosure mad in front of the chaplins tent with ceder bushes and that forms the church with the little alter in the tent inside[1]   you wished to know if i had a chance to go to confession   i did not yet but i will in the course of a week pleas God   My dear wife you asked again in your last if i wanted any mony   i have enough yet of what i brought with me and i hope we will get paid very soon   i did intend to have you send me a box with some things in it but i find that it would be only a chance if i would get it   there is hundreds of boxes sent to men here and they never get them   they get misslaid on the way and never arive   you might send me a handerchief or two by mail   any small article will come by mail and it is much shurer to come then by express   I have clothing enough now we got woolen shirts here and we got plenty towels and such things in fredericksburg   and if could have caried it we might have tobaco enough to last us three months   i seen James Burns yesterday   he is well   Leutenents and captains have no horses   they have to walk as much as the privates but they dont have so much load to cary   as for their living they buy from the brigade quartermaster and have boys to cook for them as all comissioned offisers are alowed one or more servent acording to their rank   but their is a good many of the company officers that spunge out their grub from their company and keep the mony in their pockets   but that is the fault of the sergeant to alow it   in marching they often have to get a bit of

41

grub from the company as they sometimes can not get it to buy General Meagher left here for New York on last sunday   it is rumered here that he is trying to get his brigade home to recruit it up[2]   there is another rumer that we are going to washington to do garrison dutty but there is no certainty of it   My dear wife i hope you ar spending Christmass happily   do not let your care for me fret and worry you   God is good   he brought me safe out of this last battle and he can as easily bring me safe home to you if it is his holly will   We have a rather dull Christmass here   the only extra we got was a good mess of potatoes which i am just after eating   General Meagher promised us last sunday that we would have our whisky today but we have not seen it yet   i did not taste any licquer since i joined the regiment untill last sunday   i had a little although i might of had it a good many times   i do not care for it now like i used to   i feel quite different   my constitution is stronger and i feel none of that fateiged nasty weakness that i used to feel when i was working indoors   that weary exausted feeling always made me crave for something to stimulate me but i never feel so now   i can eat anything that comes my way and feel good after it   when i get home i will not be so particular about what i eat as i used to be i can assure you   Now my dear wife i must tell you a little about the battle   on thursday morning the 11th we had revele at 4 oclock   we got up and had our breakfast got our lugage packed up left our knabsacks in camp and left some sick men to take care of them   we started about sunrise and marched about two hours   the canonading was going on all day from day-light in the morning   we lay behind the hills oppisete the citty untill evening and then we moved into a small woods and camped till morning   started again about sunrise and crossed on the pontoon bridges into fredericksburg   we lay there all day expecting to be going into the fight at any moment   when it became dark we moved our position a little and stacked arms for the night with mud ancle deep to lay down and sleep on   we hunted up pieces of boards and lay them down on the mud and then lay down and covered ourselves up in our blankets   i slept as sound i think as ever i slept in my life although our blankets were covered thick with frost in the morning   we were woke up at four oclock and

cooked our breakfast and were ready to start before daylight   every
man cooks his own grub in our company when we are out that
way as the cook was left in the camp   about eight oclock we were
ordered to fall in and we were drawn up in line of battle in one
of the streets ready to start into it at a moments notice   while we
were in that position the enemy comenced to shell us and they
done it with good efect to   they threw their shell into our line
with great precision wounding a good many   one there wounded
two men in the next file to me   the first brigade of our division
went in first[3] and in a few minutes we got the word forward   ball
and shell flying in all directions   the rebels position is on a range
of hills about a mile out side of the citty   we had to cross that
distance which is low and level with their batteries playing on us
both in front and from right and left   the storm of shell and grap
and canister was terible mowing whole gaps out of our ranks and
we having to march over their dead and wounded bodies   we advanced boldly despite it all and drove the enemy into their entrenchments but the storm of shot was then most galling and our
ranks were soon thined   our troops had to lay down to escap the
raking fire of the batteries and we had but a poor chance at the
enemy who was sheltered in his rifel pits and entrenchments   i seen
some hot work at south mountain and antetam in maryland but
they were not to be compared to this   old troops say that they
never were under such a heavy fire before in any battle   every man
that was near me in the right of the company was either killed or
wounded except one   we lost twelve in killed and wounded out of
37 men in our company   our captain was wounded in the foot
and our second leutenent was killed[4]   I have not room to write
any more in this letter but i will give more in my next   May God
bless and protect you

Your affectionate husband
PETER WELSH

1. See illustration.
2. General Meagher had obtained leave to go home to New York
to recuperate from the knee injury he had sustained at Fredericksburg.
His main object, however, was to conduct a campaign to have the bri-

gade itself come home to recruit up its strength. Meagher's efforts were of no avail. Even a personal meeting with President Lincoln could not get the Irish Brigade home, and it remained greatly under strength until the summer draft and new recruiting drives of 1863 once again began to fill up its ranks. By then General Meagher had left the brigade and returned to private life. Athearn, *Meagher*, pp. 121–25.

3. Actually, the third brigade of Hancock's division, commanded by Brig. Gen. Samuel Kosciuzko Zook, immediately preceded the Irish Brigade in the ill-fated assault on Marye's Heights at Fredericksburg. Zook's brigade was made up of the 27th Connecticut; the 2nd Delaware; 52nd, 57th, and 66th New York; and the 140th Pennsylvania. Conyngham, *Irish Brigade*, p. 342; *OR*, ser. I, vol. 21, p. 50.

4. Capt. Charles H. Sanborn was hit in the foot at Fredericksburg and went home to Boston to recuperate. 2nd Lt. John Sullivan of Co. K was killed in the same battle. Sullivan was a Milford bootmaker when he enlisted in the 28th as a sergeant on September 20, 1861. He had been commissioned second lieutenant only in September of 1862. 28th Massachusetts Monthly Report for December 1862, Mass. War Records; *Mass. Soldiers*, III 265.

Camp near Falmouth   December the 30th/62

My dear wife

i received your welcome letter of the 25th to day   i am sorry mine did not reach you sooner as it would have saved you some anxiety   i sent it on the thursday before you got it   i did not get the pilot as yet   i cant acount for my papers not coming   the two postage stamps came safe in your letter   I wrote another letter on the 25th in which i gave you some particulars of the late battle. The statement made in that letter from a soldier in this army to his mother are principly false   there has been no frost here severe enough to freeze men to death   about clothes i have never seen a man without pants nor heard of any here although i have seen some with verry raged ones   this is unavoidable in an army as large as this in a service as supplies can not always be brought forward fast enoug   as for mens living the government alows more then a man could eat if it could be got to them but that is not to be expected when the army is on a march   the full alowance of bread meat coffe and shugar is always to be had unless the wagons meet with some acident which seldom ocurs   the bread and meat alowed is not sufficient to satisfy a mans appetite without the other rations but a man can live on it   there is beans and rice and vegetables alowd   we get mixed vegetables pressed and dry which are very good to make soup[1]   Soldiers are often humbuged by the quarter-master if their sergeants do not look out for them   i have brought our quartermaster and his sergeant to the right about severel times since i been acting commisary sergeant for the company   our Colonel is the right kind of man for that   he is bound to make every man under his comand do his duty or he will know for what About laying out in the streets i gave you some acount in my last the laying on their arms is true   soldiers laying on their arms means being all night in line of battle laying down with their arms beside them ready to atack or repell the enemy at any moment   there was part of our army in this way from the day of the battle untill mon-day night when we recrossed the river   but the same troops were not on all that time   they were relieved at night   those that went on just before daylight in the morning had to remain on untill dark as they could not be relieved in the day without exposing both the

45

relief and the relieved to the fire of the enemys batteries   Sleeping
on our arms means laying down to sleep with all equipments on and
our guns either in stack in front of us or laid beside us so as to be
ready at any moment we are called up   our brigade did not have to
go to the front after the day of the battle so we escaped the un-
pleasant task of laying ten or twelve hours on the wet ground with
the certainty of having a ball whired at our head if we raised it up
that part was performed cheifly by such troops as were not engaged
in the battle and we had our full share of that   In my last i gave
you an acount of our part in the battle up to where we laid down
in front   other troops came and we soon got orders to sease firing
the officers after a while under took to take out what they could
of the brigade but they could not form in line in the position we
were in   some went out but a great many remained in front as in
going out they would be again exposed to the raking fire of the
enemys batteries   and by remaining in front we had only the fire
of infantry and sharp shuters to bear   our position was beside a
fence and a house and yard which was in our line   a great number
of our wounded were caried into that house and some of them had
to remain there untill Sunday night as our ambulance wagons could
not be brought up there   and those who had no friends to come
carry them out at night had to remain untill men were sent from
the different regiments to bring them out   I remained in front
untill dark and then brought out some wounded belonging to our
company   i went over the battle field again before daylight to see
if i could find any more of our men and the sights that were to be
seen there were hard enough   I slept about an hour that night in
the house which was being used as a hosptal in which I left the
wounded that i brought ought [out]   i cooked myself some coffe
there and then came across the river as our brigade had came across
that night   i got to the place where they had camped just as they
were falling in to go back to Fredericksburg   i reported to the
captain[2]   he was rejoiced to see me out safe   he thought i was
either killed or wounded as he came over the field early in the
action   we had only just got en[gaged when] he got wounded
he got a list from me of all the killed and wounded i knew of and
then we started and crossed over the pontoon bridge and stacked

46

arms in the firs street of the citty fronting the river   i then went to
the house where i left the wounded men i brought out to see them
i came back and told the Colonel[3] of their being there   he told me
to get men to help me and bring them over to this side to our brigade hospital   i done so and returned   we remained there in that
street that night and the next day untill after dark when we were
ordered to fall in and moved along that street on the line of the
river to the upper pontoon and came across   the troops were
brought across in good order   we had to march to this old camp
that night   the next morning the whole regiment had to go on
picket   i do not have to go on picket except when the whole company goes and then i have not to stand on post   i remain on the
reserve with the officer in comand of the company   I am very sory
for the death of our second Leutenant[4]   he was killed in the battle   in him i lost a warm friend   we have no comissond officer
belonging to the company with us now   a first leutenent of another
company has comand since our Captain went home[5]   the first Leut
belong to the company resighned in september[6] and the one who
was second Leut has been away since august   he got wounded but
he is well now   he has been promoted to first Leut but he has not
come back yet[7]   My dear wife you say you want to send me some
things   i mentioned in my last that i did not want you to send me
a box as it is only a chance if i would get it   but you could send
me any small article by mail done up in a wrapper   there is one
thing i wish you would send me that is some salve ointment   you
might sew it up in a little bag make it flat and fold it up in a
handerchief and send it   It is very hard to keep clear of vermin
here as on comes in contact with those who are dirty and cannot
avoid it   My dear wife there is not room for any more in this
so i must come to a close praying God to bless and protect you

Your loving husband
PETER WELSH

1. During most of the war the daily food allowance for Union soldiers
was "twelve ounces of pork or bacon, or, one pound and four ounces of
salt or fresh beef; one pound and six ounces of soft bread or flour, or,
one pound of hard bread, or, one pound and four ounces of corn meal;

and to every one hundred rations, fifteen pounds of beans or peas, *and* ten pounds of rice or hominy; ten pounds of green coffee, or, eight pounds of roasted (or roasted and ground) coffee, or, one pound and eight ounces of tea; fifteen pounds of sugar; four quarts of vinegar; . . . three pounds and twelve ounces of salt; four ounces of pepper; thirty pounds of potatoes, when practicable, and one quart of molasses." The dried vegetables (desiccated vegetables) to which Welsh refers were not popular with many soldiers, and were often referred to as "desecrated vegetables." "The only practical means of using the mixture was in soup." Wiley, *Billy Yank*, pp. 224, 242.

2. Capt. Charles H. Sanborn.

3. Col. Richard Byrnes.

4. 2nd Lt. John Sullivan.

5. Cannot identify.

6. John Ahern was a boot treer in Milford, Massachusetts when he was mustered into the 28th on December 13, 1861 as a first lieutenant. He resigned and was discharged on September 23, 1862. *Mass. Soldiers*, III 259.

7. John Killian was a 22-year-old carpenter from Roxbury when he was commissioned second lieutenant in the 28th on December 3, 1861. He was promoted to first lieutenant July 27, 1862, but was wounded at the battle of Second Bull Run, August 30, 1862 and never returned to the 28th. He was discharged for his wounds February 14, 1863. *Mass. Soldiers*, III 262.

1863

"IS THIS NOT WORTH FIGHTING FOR?"

PETER WELSH did not see as much action in the whole of 1863 as he had in the last few months of 1862. The Irish Brigade was so reduced in numbers that it could not be the fighting force that it had been the previous year. At Chancellorsville in the spring it was kept back from most of the action until May 3rd, when it showed some of its old flair in its successful effort to rescue the 5th Maine Battery from capture by the Confederates. At Gettysburg, the brigade saw its hardest fighting of the year when it was hotly engaged around Little Round Top and in the wheatfield on the second day of the battle. The fall saw the brigade take part in the Bristoe and Mine Run campaigns, but for the brigade, as for the army as a whole, these campaigns produced few losses and even fewer real gains.

Though a soldier lives to fight, his time is mostly occupied by other matters. 1863 was a not uneventful year for Peter Welsh. The high point of his career as a soldier came on March 17, 1863. On that day the brigade held one of its famous St. Patrick's Day celebrations. Attended by General Hooker and other dignitaries, the festivities included horse races and other competitions for the men, followed by theatricals, recitations, songs, and toasts that lasted well into the night. At one point in the evening, however, some skirmishing up the river interrupted the revelry and the brigade was ordered to fall in without a moment's delay. When the 28th's color bearer failed to produce the regiment's green flag, Peter Welsh was sent to find it. The negligent color bearer had lost his post, for when

Welsh returned with the flag his captain told him to keep it. The regimental commander confirmed the new appointment the following day. Despite Margaret's misgivings, Peter vowed to "carry it as long as God gives me strength," for, as he later told his father-in-law, he felt "proud to bear that emblem of Ireland's pride and glory."

Exactly what carrying the flag meant to Welsh was spelled out in his correspondence during the year. In his idle hours in camp during 1863 he had time to think through the meaning of the war and the Irishman's place in it. He expressed no fears for his own safety, but left his fate in God's hands. He wrote of the importance of preserving the Union as an asylum for the oppressed people of Ireland. He reminded Margaret of the many benefits America had bestowed on the sons and daughters of Erin and suggested to his father-in-law the possible benefits to Ireland itself of a Union victory. Most of all he defended America as a place where the masses might prosper. "Contrast the condition of the masses of any other country in the world," he told Margaret, "and the advantages we enjoy will stand out boldly so that the blindest can see them." Even the poorest could aspire to "all the honours and the highest position that a great nation can bestow." "And," he passionately concluded, "is this not worth fighting for?"

Camp near Falmouth   January the 4th/63

My dear wife

It is sunday evening   all the duties of the day are over except roll call which we have at 8 ½ P M   Our duties on sunday consist of inspection in the forenoon and dress parade at sun set   the regular routine of camp life is roll call at sunrise then breakfast the drum beats at half past seven for Doctors call   all the sick who are not in hospidal must go to the doctors tent at that time and have their complaints attended to   if the doctor thinks any of them to sick for duty he can excuse them from duty and they will not have anything to do on that day   a great many go and make a long face and play sick when there is scarcely anything the matter with them   the doctors see so much of that work that it is hard for a man who is realy sick to get excused unless his disability is very aparent   The next thing that comes is turn out the men that are detailed for picket guard or fateiuge   then we have company drill from ten to eleven Oclock   come in then and have diner at twelve   the next is Batalion drill at three which at which [sic] the whole regiment is out   it generly lasts about an hour and a half then at sun set dress parade   at dress parade the regiment is drawn up in line in front of the camp and the Colnel put us through the manual of arms and if their is any general orders or any regimental orders the Ajutant reads them to the regiment after which we return to our quarters   dress parade does not ocupy more then fifteen or twenty minutes   then we have supper do as we please from then untill roll call after which we may go to bed as soon as we please taps are beat about half an hour after roll call for to put out the lights but a man may sit at the fire as long as he likes if he wishes to   I have very comfortable quarters now and plenty of candle light as we have only two lights to keep going out of the company alowance as all the company except the orderly sergeant and me and the cook are in the one building   we sleep in the cook house which we have built of logs and the joints plastered with mud   the chimney is built of the same material   the roof is covered with poles then a coat of cedar boughs and a coat of mud on top of that   our bed is riged up on four forked sticks and poles laid lenghtways   a coat of ceder boughs on them and an army bed tick that some of the boys caried from fredericksburg we have filled with dry leaves   the first two nights we lay on it we could not sleep we were so unused to anything in the shape of a bed   the only trouble with our shanty is that the chimney smokes a little sometimes   it reminds us of the old story of the smokey chimney and the scolding wife   if a vote of choice was taken the scolding wife would cary a unanemious vote here   there is many a man here that would give his hat and boots he would for just to be beside her   i do not belong to that class myself   i would like to be beside my own little wife as much as any man but my reasons for so wishing are different from those i have reference to   men who have neither life soul nor energy enough for any position or profession in life have no business here   they are useless to the army and a misery to themselves   there is men in this army who would except any condition of life to get out of the service and the majority of them are men who never were as well of in their lives before   they hate to do any duty no matter how light   if it were not for the decipline that compells them more then half of them would die for want of exercise   a great many of those have enlisted because they thought they would be clothed and fed and have a lazy time   the shurest way to preserve health here is to keep busy at something   plenty of exercise is the best medicine in the army   this is plain to be seen   the constant exposure to night air damp ground to lay on at night and exposure to the enclemency of the weather must cause disease of varies kinds if the blood is not kept in good circulation   bathing the head in cold water every morning is of great service to keep the sistem in a healthy condition that is a performance i go through every morning unless when suden marching orders prevent me   Their is a good many of our regiment who hate our Colnel because he is a man of decipline he is the right kind of an officer to have comand   he will alow neither Officers nor men to shirk their duty   there is no partiality shown to any   he also looks out for the rights of his regiment   if there is any cause of complaint he makes it his buisness to look after it imediately   we have clothing in abundance now   we got wollen gloves and legans since christmass and we all got gansie[1] jackets today   They came very near moving us from here a few days ago but the order was countermanded   a part of this army

52

went on a reconoicence up the river but they all returned   but there is no certainety of how long we will remain here   one thing is pretty certain that they do not intend to atack the enemy in the same place again as it would cost to much even should it prove sucsessfull   this is something they should of known before the atemt was made and had McClellen[2] been in comand i am certain he would not have atemted to take the works behind Fredericksburg by the same means that Burnside[3] did   i do not think for a moment that the enemy could not have been driven from his position with the means and men which Burnside had at his comand had the atack been properly conducted   but the whole plan was a failure except the crossing and recrossing the river which was well done   i do not want to ever get into such an afair as that again   i am willing to run my risk in any way or any where that by doing so i can be of service but to run the risk and and [sic] when you get as far as you can go and see that all you can do is useless is a dull business   a comission gulentine [guillotine] is much needed by which all inefecient comissions should be beheaded and men from the ranks put in their place   My dear wife i sent you a letter on tuesday the same day i received your last letter   i must now come to a close hoping this may find you in good health and in better spirits then you have been of late   begin the new year with the determination of keeping up your spirits   God is good and i will be with you before very long with his blessing

your afectionate husband
PETER WELSH

1. Probably "gawsy," a word of Scottish origin meaning "large and handsome." *Oxford English Dictionary*, IV 86.

2. George Brinton McClellan (1826–1885), youthful, handsome, and brilliant, the first and most popular commander of the Army of the Potomac, was one of the most controversial figures of the war. His rise was meteoric. Well prepared by a West Point education (1846), field experience in the Mexican War, and deep study of both American and European military systems, McClellan made the Army of the Potomac into a spirited, well-disciplined organization. He was always popular with his troops, but his over-cautious pursuit of the enemy in the

Peninsula and Maryland campaigns of 1862 led to his removal by Lincoln in November of that year. There was bitterness in the army over his removal, especially in the Irish Brigade where he was a great favorite, but he never again held field command. He ran unsuccessfully against Lincoln for the presidency in 1864. *DAB.*

3. Ambrose Everett Burnside's (1824–1881) tenure as a commander of the Army of the Potomac was short and undistinguished. He assumed command at Lincoln's request after McClellan was removed in November of 1862 and was himself relieved after the fiasco at Fredericksburg and the infamous mud march of January 1863, in which the entire army bogged down in the rain-soaked roads of northern Virginia. Burnside was physically imposing and had a pleasing personality, but his talents for high command were limited. To his credit, he recognized this fact, tried to avoid Lincoln's entreaties to take over the army, and accepted full responsibility for his eventual failures. He continued to hold important positions in the army for the rest of the war after his removal from command of the Army of the Potomac. *DAB.*

Camp near Falmouth   January the 7th/63

My dear wife

i received your welcom letter of the 1st on the 5th   i had posted
a letter to you that morning   i am glad that you seem to be in
better spirits   be of good cheer my dear wife and all will yet be
well with the blessing of God   we do not know here where we will
go to when we move nor when we will move   that is something that
our comanding officers dont know untill they get the order to march
We have very fine weather here   there was a light fall of snow in
the early part of December and some cold weather but that did not
last long   there has been very little rain here this winter as yet
The kind of handerchiefs i want is a couple of dark colored cotton
pocket handerchiefs   i received the pilot with your last letter   it
was a great treat as i had not got one for so long before   newsmen
bring dayly papers here but they charge ten cents for a New York
heareld and five cents for a Philadelphia paper   i do not know
whether they have been stopped of late or not but i have not seen
any around here for several days   it is reported that the rebels got
considerable information by getting newspapers from our pickets
all communication with the enemys pickets is prohibeted now   I
seen James Burns last night   he is well and in good spirits   My
dear wife just imagine you see me now   i am sitting beside the fire
on a cracker box   a box in which the company books are caried
placed on the end of our bed forms a desk to write on   the cook
is buisy cooking beef soup for diner   the orderly sergeant is sitting
on the cooks bed looking over some tactics of drill   now imagine
you see the inside of a long shanty with a big fireplace at one end
some cracker boxes nailed against the wall for closets and shelves
three rifles standing in one corner canteens belts and catridge boxes
hanging against the wall and you can form a good idea of the general apearence of the interior of our quarters   it is however a
luxury compared with living in a little shelter tent   i have just
been disturbed by having to give the cook the cracker box i was sitting on to put our beef in   he cuts it up in that and and [sic] then
i give it out to the men as their names are called   i must postpone
finishing my letter untill afternoon as the quartermasters sergeant
has just been here to tell me that he is ready to issue two days

rations   It is one oclock rations drawn and my diner eat   i feel purty fair   i had a good mess of soup for dinner   we had dry pressed vegatables and onions which make very good soup   it would make you laugh to see us cook our grub when we are marching and every man has to cary his grub with him and cook for himself[:] to see every man with his tin dipper boiling his coffe and frying meat on a tin plate   when we have a chance to get any flour or indian meal we make flap jacks   i have made many a mess of them and they go good for a change   we canot get any flour or meal here   when the corn was standing in the fields we used to pull the ears and grind them to meal by punching holes in a piece of tin and rubing the ear of corn on the rough side of it   thus by a goodeal of labour one could get a good mess of meal and it is quite a treat when one has been a long time on hard bread   the hard bread we get is with few exceptions very good and situated as we are it is much better for men then soft bread   i would get tired of soft bread when i could not get vegetables but i can eat the hard bread any time when marching   i eat a cracker or two every time we halt to rest and you have no idea how one will relish a dry cracker without anything with it   My dear wife it is drawing near the time for our Batalion drill   ha the drum is beating   i must start   Well drill is over   the day being clear and cool drilling is but exercise enough to keep us comfortably warm   the soup caught particular fits when we got on the double quick   And now my dear wife i dont know as i have anything more to write at present that would interest you   let me know in your next how James Gleason is getting on if he has plenty of work and also how your uncle and James are getting along   give my love to them all   good by   God bless and protect you

your affectionate husband
PETER WELSH

In camp near Falmouth   January the 14th/63

My dear wife

i received your welcome letter on the 12th   the postage stamps and the parcel came safe   i am very glad you sent me the Agnes Dei[1]   i have got it on my neck   the handerchief is just the kind i want but i would like the other one a little smaller sise as i have a small pocket to carry it in   the ointment came all right   i would not take ten dollars for it   i tried every means to get some before i thought of having you send it to me   i might of had i [it] along agone if i had thought of sending to you for it   all that is necessary is for me to carry it about me and i wear a mony belt in which i can cary it without any trouble   Situated as i am now i can keep clear of such dirt easy enough   but when we are marching and sleeping in shelter tents it is impossible to keep clear of them when there is any men in the company who are dirty and when marching we have no time to wash our cloths   and even if we had time to wash if they get on to you it is necessary to chang all your cloths at the same time which soldiers cannot allways do for they do not have cloths enough to do it   We are well suplied with clothing now but if we started on a march some of the men would not have half of their clothing after a couple of weeks   some throw them away when they get tired carrying them and others when their under cloths get dirty throw them away through laziness to wash them   James Burns not wounded   he is well   i would not have written that he came out safe if he was wounded   i went over to his quarters as soon as i got your letter and told him   he said he had written home twice since the battle   It is useless to make any calculations about our moving or where we might be sent   whether this brigade remains here or not it is quite evident from the orders read to us on dress parade last night that they mean to keep this army here for some time   we do not want to move unless they send us where there is good garrison quarters for we have a good camp here   all officers and men from other regiments who see our camp say we have the best quarters and cleanest camp of any regiment in this army   My dear wife you do not mention how you are getting your health now i hope you are in better health then you were   be of good cheer for we will be happy together yet with the blessing of God   my health is good thank God and i am hearty and strong give my love to all our friends   I hope the paymaster will soon come round so that i can send you some money   i thought i would been able to send you some before this   i think however that we will get paid very soon now   I must conclude praying God to bless and protect you

your affectionate husband

PETER WELSH

1. The Agnus Dei (Latin for "Lamb of God") to which Welsh refers was probably a medallion stamped with the figure of a lamb with a halo and cross, an ecclesiastical symbol emblematic of Christ.

In Camp near Falmouth   January 23d/63

My dear wife

i have been expecting a letter from you for several days but did not get any   we got paid up to the first of November on last sunday that mad my share 25 dollars   i sent you 20 dollars by the Priest of the 88th[1]   he he [sic] came over here to take up a subscription to get a new set of vestments i gave him one dollar   that left me four dollars to keep but we had a regular jolification here so i spent my four dollars and i want you to send me one dollar the next time you write to me   that will do me i hope untill we get paid again as we are mustered in for two months more pay which we will get when the rest of the brigade get paid   We have had wet weather here all this week   the army got started to move and had to stop the roads got so bad   we had orders to be ready but we were to wait in our camp untill the rest of the army got ahead of us as we are to fall in the rear[2]   the mony was sent by express so you will have got it before you get this   i will write to you very soon again and hoping this may find you in good health as it leaves me at present thank God   i will conclude by praying God to bless and protect you

your affectionate husband
PETER WELSH

1. Rev. William Corby, c.s.c.

2. This was the infamous mud march of the Army of the Potomac. On January 16th Burnside ordered the army to prepare for a new offensive, and on the 20th they broke camp and prepared to push south. But heavy downpours turned the roads to mire so deep that it was impossible for the men to move. "It became a question of getting them extricated and back to their quarters, rather than one of striking the enemy," observed an officer from the 116th Pennsylvania. Luckily for Peter Welsh and the Irish Brigade, the Second Corps was the last to move and, as a consequence, they never had to leave their quarters. They took "great consolation in the fact, especially when they saw the condition of the bedraggled infantry and mud-covered artillery, that was once hub-deep in the sea of liquid clay that was once a road." St. Clair A. Mulholland, *Story of the 116th Regiment Pennsylvania Volunteers* (Philadelphia: McManus, 1903), pp. 72–73.

In camp near Falmouth   January the 27th/63

My dear wife

I received your welcome letter of the 20th this morning   the handerchief came safe   it is just what i wanted   it will last me untill i get home i hope   the postage stamps came safe and just in time for i had none   I sent you a letter on the 23d in which i told you that i sent you twenty dollars by the chaplin of the 88th   i gave it to him on the 19th and he was to send it by express so that you must have got it before this   i gave him one dollar towards getting his new vestments   our regiment acted very liberal with him   he must have got as much as $250 from us   we had a jolly time here for a couple of days after we got paid and we wanted something for to raise a little life and fun for the time grows dull when we are a long one plac without anything ocuring to create an excitement   it is all over ecept that a few of the boys are in the guard house yet for getting drunk and being noisey and for stopping away from camp   there is nearly three months more pay due to us now we have been mustered in for two months and i hope we will soon be paid so that i can send you some more   the four months that the regiment was paid for was from the division that we were in before we joind the Irish brigade   I suppose there is a great many rumers in the papers about the movements of of [sic] this army but the army is stuck pretty fast for the present   the roads are in such a condition that it is impossible to move the army at present and there is little prospect of them getting better as the rainy season is comenced here   we will get along very well if they leave us here which i think they will have to for a while   you mentioned that they are talking of joining the small regiments together   it is what they should do if they mean to keep them in the field but our regiment is to large for that   although we have not many here there is a great many in hospital who will be able to do duty when they get well of their slight wounds   My dear wife i am sory to hear that you are so nervous   you must go to a doctor and get something to do you good   it will not do for you to neglect it   I am in good health thank God and i hope with his blessing that you will soon be in good health to   above all things take good care of your health and leave nothing undone that would serve it   give my love to James Gleason and Ann and to your uncle and aunt and James   i have no news worth writing at present so i must bid you good by for the present with praying all the blessings of heaven upon you

your affectionate husband

PETER WELSH

[Fragment, ca. February 1863][1]

I see by late papers that the govener of Massachusets has been autheured to raise nigar regiments   i hope he may suceed but it doubt it very much   if they can raise a few thousand and send them out here i can asure you that whether they have the grit to go into battle or not if they are placed in front and any brigade of this army behind them they will have to go in or they will meet as hot a reception in their retreat as in their advance   The feeling against nigars is intensly strong in this army as is plainly to be seen wherever and whenever they meet them   They are looked upon as the principal cause of this war and this feeling is especialy strong in the Irish regiments[2]   This however is not wholey true for there is numerous circumstances conected with this war which go to prove that had slavery not existed the promoters and instagaters of this war would have seised on some other question and used it as a bone of contention by which they could keep up agitation and distract the minds of the people both north and south untill it would finely result in civel war   George Washington warned his country men to beware of foreighn influence   they have been warned many times since to beware and especialy of the hipocritacal intrieuging of that acursed harlot of nations England   but the warnings were only laughed at   It was in England that the agitation of the slavery question was first comenced and thousands of pounds contributed to keep it up and for what   was it for the benifit of the negro   her conduct towards this country since the comencment of this war answers that question plainly   her whole course has been in aid of the rebels just as far as she could without comiting herself to a war with this goverment   her object is and has been for years to divide this country and thereby destroy her power and greatness all monarchial powers hate republics but that perfedious tyrant hipocrite cut throat murderess and base usurper of both church and state hates this country for two reasons   first for her liberal goverment and laws and second because America was out riviling her both in power comerce and manufacture   Eighty years ago what was the condition of the lower classes in England or in any of her colonies   and what were the laws by which they were crushed and trampled on her history tells, and what compelled her to grant

62

more liberal ones   the establishment of this republic   as it grew in
strenght its influence has compelled her to grant more liberal laws
and in other nations it had the same efect   but if it should now
fall then away with all hope of liberty in europe and particularly
for poor old Erin [breaks off, incomplete]

1. This fragment has no date or addressee. The dating is approximate,
being based on the reference to the governor of Massachusett's authori-
zation to raise Negro troops. On January 26, 1863, Gov. John Andrew
was authorized by Secretary of War Edwin M. Stanton to raise volunteer
infantry units which "may include persons of African descent, organized
into separate corps." *OR*, ser. III, vol. 3, pp. 20–21.

2. Peter Welsh's observations are confirmed by Bell Irvin Wiley. He
noted that "One who reads letters and diaries of Union soldiers en-
counters an enormous amount of antipathy toward Negroes." And, he
added, the Irish were particularly steeped in racial prejudice even before
entering the service. *Billy Yank*, p. 109.

In camp near Falmouth   February the 3d/63

My dear wife

i received your welcome letter of the 30th to day   i am sory that you gave yourself any trouble about the mony   it was done up in an envelope and adressed so that it would go to the house to you   i have got a receipt from Adams express for the mony   I would not have troubled the chaplin to send it if i could do it myself but i could not as the express company have no agent here nor do they cary anything here   they cary to and from Aquia creek which is some eight or ten miles frome here   articals sent by express for any one here are caried there and brought from there by the quartermasters to their regiments   the chaplin of the 88th told us that he had a pass to go to Aquia creek and that he was going in two or three days and that he would send home mony for any of us that wished as he sends home mony for the men of his own regiment in the same way   i cannot tell you the chaplins name at present as i never enquired what his name is   but i will find out   the receipt i have was dated at Washington the 27th of January so that the mony could scarcely have reached you on the morning of the 30th but it is entirely safe   The men who are sending their mony to Massachusets give it back to the paymaster   their names are sighned on a roll and forwarded to the state treasurer and he sends the mony to their friends at home   but that can not be done in the case of sending mony to a state other then the one the regiment belongs to[1] I got your last letter and the handerchief safe   i wrote you a letter on the same day   My dear wife i hope you will try and look at our situation in a different light   i know that it is hard for you and that you must feel lonesome and it is also hard for me to be so long seperated from you   it is the only worldly care or trouble i have all the hardships and inconvenience of a soldiers life do not trouble me in the least   while it is Gods will to grant me health and strenght i shall have nothing to regret but being seperated from you so long But now my dear wife if you will just come with me a few moments into the merits of the case we will see on what grounds we stand   In the first place you know how it was and under what circumstances i volunteered   i did not come here against the dictates of my conscience for i would have been into this long before   i [It] was

64

only that i did not want to be away from you and that you would
be lonesome and fretting about me that kept me to home and
would have kept me out of this altogether had not that unfortunate
trip to Boston ocured   you kno the rest   how after i had got on the
spree and spent all the mony i had with me the shame and remorse
i felt for what i had done made me wish to be out of sight of
everyone i ever knew   But there is always a cause for everything
and the amediate cause of my coming here is no more then one
grain of sand to all on the sea shore compared with the cause in
which we are engaged   i know that you look at those things in a
differen way from what i do but take the whole subject and take a
calm just view of it and see if every one of us have not a special
interest in the result   In the first place rebellion without a just
cause is a crime of the greatest magnitude   we have St Paul for
autherity   he says that he who unjustly rebells rebells against the
will of God and draws upon himself eternal damnation   did the
rebels have a just cause, no   although the fanitics of the north
were the agressors by their party platforms and agitation yet no
man of sound just judgement will say that was a sufficient cause for
armed rebellion   for a decision of this question you have only to
refer to the political doctrine of Arch Bishop Hughs[2] one whose
abilitys as a statesman as well as an eclisastic are second to none in
the land   you may say what is it to me   let them fight it out between themselves   this i know is said by many but who are they!
this is my country as much as the man that was born on the soil and
so it is with every man who comes to this country and becomes a
citezen   this being the case i have as much interest in the main-
tenence of the goverment and laws and the integrity of the nation
as any other man   and even to those who are not citezens nor have
not joined the service of the goverment in this war the integrity of
this nation is a matter of the greatest importance   this war with all
its evils with all its erors and missmanagement is a war in which the
people of all nations have a vital interest   this is the first test of a
modern free government in the act of sustaining itself against internal enemys and matured rebellion   all men who love free government and equal laws are watching this crisis to see if a republic
can sustain itself in such a case   if it fail then the hopes of milions

fall and the desighns and wishes of all tyrants will suceed   the old cry will be sent forth from the aristocrats of europe that such is the comon end of all republics   the blatent croakers of the devine right of kings will shout forth their joy   the giant republic has fallen   That there has been the grossest missmanagement and fraud caried on by oficials politecians and intreguers in the conduct of this war i willingly admit and that there is disatisfaction and loud denunciation of the course of the executive in the army with the course pursued in the slavery question   but if slavery is in the way of a proper administration of the laws and the integrity and perpetuety of this nation then i say away with both slaves and slavery   sweep both from the land forever rather then the freedom and prosperity of a great naion such as this should be destroyed   A great nation i fancy i hear you say   what better off are we here then we were at home   we always had enough to eat and respectable raiment at home and good oppertunitys for enjoyment   that being true in your case does not make it so for others   how many thousands are there in this country who saw nothing but opression and misery at home who are now in comfort or if not in comfort in nine cases out of ten it is their own fault   what would be the condition to day of hundreds of thousands of the sons and daughters of poor opressed old erin if they had not a free land like this to emigrate to   famine and misery staring them in the face and that famine not the result of any extraordinary falure in the products of the soil but the result of tyranical laws and damnable opression   the same may be said of thousands from other lands and especialy of the opressed states of jermany   but on no other spot on the face of the earth was such tyrany and treachery practised as in Irland by its vilianous rulers   Contrast the condition of the masses of this with any other country in the world and the advantages we enjoy will stand out boldly so that the blindest can see them   Here there is no bloated peted [petted] rascals or what is called in monarchial countrys the aristocracy   if we have an aristocracy it must be self made and consequently can be of little injury to the interests of the masses compared with where it is upheld by law and is part and parcel of the goverment and whether just or unjust fools or wise men scoundrels or gentlemen take their place by law as rulers of

66

the people   thank God we have none of that here and God grant for the sake of the relieous as well as political liberty of coming generations that there never will   Here the poorest mother may look with joy and satisfaction on her ofspring if she only gives him a proper training in his tender years[—]that is the all important point[—]and from that [he] takes his start with all the honours and the hiest position that a great nation can bestow open before him And is this not worth fiting for   i fancy i hear some one say those who fight for it are not the ones who will reap the benefit of it   that may be true with the majority but what is our relation to our fellow men   for what were we sent here in a relegious point   we all know that to gain the salvation of our souls is the all inportant object   but we have political relation with our felow man and it is our duty to do our share for the comon wellfare not only of the present generation but of future generations   such being the case it becomes the duty of every one no matter what his position to do all in his power to sustain for the present and to perpetuate for the benefit future generations a goverment and a national asylum which is superior to any the world has yet known   One of the most important yes the most important of all rights enjoyed by the citezen of a free nation is the liberty of concience   free alters is an invaluable boon and where on earth except in that fountain of religion Rome can any one point out to me a spot where the Church enjoys such fredom as in the United States   not even in Catholic France for there the religious press is bridled and her first Bishops are silenced   not in that most Catholic of Catholic nations Austria for there the church is hampered by tenporal laws   But i must stop for want of space   i might write for a week on the subject before me and not do it half justice   But there is yet something in this land worth fighting for

Your loving husband
PETER WELSH

The dollar and stamps came safe   I seen James Burns last night he is well   give my love to our friends

1. Chap. 62 of the *Acts and Resolves . . . 1862* (Boston: White, 1862) allowed the treasurer and receiver-general to receive and distribute

money remitted by Massachusetts volunteers in the manner Peter Welsh describes.

2. John Joseph Hughes (1797–1864) was Coadjutor (1838), Bishop (1842), and then first Archbishop (1850) of New York. Born in Ireland, he came to the United States as an uneducated laborer after the War of 1812. He was ordained a priest in 1826 and quickly rose in the Church on the strength of his fierce defense of the Irish-Catholic immigrant against nativist assaults. Under Hughes, Catholic churches and institutions flourished, and Irish-Americans throughout the country came to regard him as their spokesman. Though not an advocate of black emancipation, he firmly rejected the right of secession and staunchly supported the Union cause until his death in 1864. *DAB*.

In camp near Falmouth   February the 8th/63

My dear wife

i received your welcome letter of the 30th stating that you had received the mony   i am glad you got it so soon for i know you felt uneasy about it but i knew it was safe   I received your letter in which you sent me the dollar and postage stamps on the third and i wrote you a letter the same evening   My dear wife i hope you are getting better health and if not do not neglect to go to some good doctor and try to get something to do you good   I am in exelant health thank God   i weighed myself this morning and i weighed more than ever i did before   i am fifteen pounds heavier then i was a year agone   We had a snow storm here a few days ago but it is all gone now and the weather is very fine but terafirma is all mud and pudle   there is some talk here that we are to move back near Washington but there is no certainety of it   the ninth army core moved away from here on friday   i do not know where they have gone   it is my opinion that all this army will be moved from here very soon   they cannot make any advance in this direction during the winter season   They are discharging all the sick and disabled men here who are not fit for duty   there is a good many of those that came out last sumer getting their discharge   they are principly old men and should never been taken into the service Dear wife you must excuse me for continueing to send you this kind of paper and envelopes[1]   i could not get any other but will send plain ones as soon as i can get them   I wish you would let me know in your next if you have heard from my sister or from home lately My dear wife i wrote you a long letter the last one in which i aduced a few of the many reasons why we should still stand true and firm in the cause of the nation   I am as much disgusted with the management of this unfortunate war as any one can be   i know that political fraud and trickery is the principal cause of our disasters that through party influence incompetent parties are placed in positions of trust and danger where none but the most tried and trusty should be placed   jealousy between our leading Generals as to who shall be the leading man has been of great injury in this war and brought on some of our worst defeats   But this is a world of changes there is nothing stationary in it and this is particularly a country of changes which is the natural result of its form of government hence the men who are leaders to day may not be leaders tomorow and in consequence of such frequent changes as are unavoidable from the internal convulsion through which the country is passing the right man must eventualy find himself in the right place   And then we may look for quick and shure work for war like fire is a great purifier   the cost of this war in blood and treasure the misery and grief it has cost the country must bring the people to a true sense of their position   and inspite of the imbecility of an incompetent administration and fanatical nigar worshippers a people great and free as the people of this country are will rise in their might and power with their eyes opened by bitter experience and trample in the dust any and everything that stands in the way of puting a sucesfull termination to this acursed rebellion   and although slaves and slavery abolitionests and and [sic] their isms should be swept from the land swept from the land [sic] they both will be if they stand in the way of the peace and prosperity of the country   This war is undoubtebly a just chastisement of the hand of God the recklessness and luxury of some and the disapation and debauchery of others the political swindling and fraud and the general low moral standard of a very large class of the American people   the last i believe to be the result of the publick school sistem as caried out in the majority of cases where there is neither releigous training nor morality taught either by practice or precept those evils i believe has brought this war as a chastisement on the country and blive me it will be a powerfull purifier   Give my love to all our friends   God bless and protect you

your affectionate husband
PETER WELSH

I seen James Burns at Mass today   he is well

---

1. The stationery on which this letter was written had a one-and-one-half-inch oval picture of the United States flag at the top left, and on the right a ten-line poem entitled "Our Country's Flag." Under the picture was the motto "One Flag and One Government." (See illustration.) Evidently Margaret Welsh had objected to patriotic stationery bearing General McClellan's likeness. (See illustration.)

In camp near Falmouth   February the 15th/63

My dear wife

I have not received a letter from you since the sixth   that was the one stating that you had received the mony   i received the one before that on the third and sent you one on the fourth   i sent you another on the ninth   i have been anxiously expecting one from you but did not get one   I hope that you are getting good health and better spirits   i am in excelant health thank God   We have very mild weather here now but it rains often enough to keep the roads in a constant pudle   General Meagher has returned here and our captain[1] has got back and brought a new green flag for the regiment   There is nothing of any interest transpiring here at present   we still hear rumers of falling back to washington to take the place of some brigade that has not done any fighting yet but that is all we know about it   I seen James Burns last night   he is well   he says he is going to try to get a furlough to go home   My dear wife i have not much to write untill i hear from you which i hope will be very soon   give my love to James Gleason and Ann to your uncle and aunt and James   Be of good cheer Margaret   our destiny is in the hand of God and his will be done   i have no fears for i know that he can protect us anywhere no matter how danger-ous our position   our days are numbered and we must fill them that is an unalterable decree which no power on earth can change this being the case we have nothing to do but make the best use we can of our time and with an unwavering faith place our trust in him for the rest   The folly with which some people talk about those who lose their lives in war or other dangers is surprising especialy in Catholics when our relegion teaches so different   a man may bring sickness trials and misery upon himself by his own acts but he can as easily create himself as destroy his own life if his time is not full   and so in relation to others   he canot destroy the life of another no more then he could create him if it was not by the will of the creater that the others time was at that moment to end   This is a decree over which we have no control   it is possible that we might by our own acts have changed the place the maner and cause but there is always some cause and the result folows which is un-alterable   Thus by the will of God we will be happy together again i hope and that before very long   may God bless and protect you

your affectionate husband

PETER WELSH

1. Capt. Charles H. Sanborn had been at home in Boston while re-
covering from wounds received at the battle of Fredericksburg, December 13, 1862. 28th Massachusetts Monthly Report for December 1862
and 28th Massachusetts Monthly Report for January 1863, Mass. War
Records.

In camp near Falmouth   February the 22nd/63

My dear wife

I received your welcome letter of the sixteenth on yesterday   i was begining to feel very uneasy   i was so long without hearing from you   i sent a letter to you on the fifteenth   Dear wife i can relieve your anxiety about me going to confession   i was to confession last night and received holy Comunion to day   thank God for his goodness in alowing me to aproach his holy sacraments once more   I resolved to go at woncet as there is a report here that the three old regiments of the brigade are going away and other troops coming to take their place[1]   in that case we would be left without a chaplin[2]   but whether there is any truth in this report or not i cannot say   i hope the whole brigade will be left together whether they go or stay   Dear wife i am sory to hear from you that you do not care what St Paul or Bishop Hughes says   you must look at things in a spiritual as well as temporal light   if it were my misfortune to be disabled or loose an arm or leg which God forbid then i should accept it as the will of God and consider it was for the best for there is not a misfortune in the whole catalogue of human calamitys which if thoroughly investigated will not produce positive evidence that it was for the spiritual benifit of the indevedual to whom it happened   No doubt but the majority of those who get maimed in this war will have but a poor chance to make a living but what cignify a few years of hardship and poverty if that should be the means of gaining that souls salvation   Prosperity and sucess generly leads us from God while poverity and hardship makes us turn to our creater and look up to him for help and aid   it withdraws our attachments from this world and the things that are in it and makes us look to another world for that peace and happiness which is denied us here   My dear wife you tell me to look back at the time since we were maried and see how many happy days you have spent   i am well aware that i have caused you many a days weeks and months of unhappiness   God forgive me for it and many a days grief it has given me   but with Gods blessing when i return i will try to make amends for the past   You need not fear that i will needlessly expose myself to danger   that would be foolish and useless but i am determined to do my duty   i have sworn to serve faithfully and with Gods blessing i will keep that oath   You say you do not think God has anything to do with this war for the priests and Bishops are devided on it as well as the people   but that is nothing new   such diversity of opinion ocurs between the hierarchy in most all wars   such was the case in every revelution that has ocured in Irland   it was so in the Rusian war and it was even so when the two most Catholic of nations France and Austria were at war   and is it not so to day in Italy where a great many of the clergy in the dominion of Sardenia are opposed to the temperal power of the Pope   The clergy being devided upon the war question does not therefore go to prove that God has nothing to do with it   God in his justice alows evil men to ferment discord and precipitate nations into war with each other and the people of the same nation against each other as a chastisement for their ofences against his devine laws   and he has even alowed nations who were great and prosperous to become extinct through being conqured by other nations as a chastisement for their unritiousness and infidelity   My dear wife you tell me of the admonition of the fathers of fifty ninth St[3] that dying on the battlefield will not save a mans soul unless he is in a state of grace   shurely no Catholic is so silly or so ignorant of the teachings of the Catholic church as to believe that dying on the battle field would gain their salvation   You say there is not a word about the poor felows who sacrifised their lives at fredericksburg no more then if they never lived   but there is just as much about them as there is about those who die at home   how long are any remembered after death has snatched them in his cold embrace except indeed in a very few cases where on loses the nearest and dearest to them on earth   but outside of this they are soon forgotten   ones friends indeed give him a cold winding sheat and folow him to the grave with a solem face   but that over they go back into the gay world and the departed one is thought no more of I would be most happy to get a furlow if i could but there is no chance   there has not one enlisted man got a furlow from this regiment except some who were at hospital wounded and no furlows will be got untill the Colonel comes back   and the order to grant furlows of ten days to two men out of every hundred at a time may be recinded by that time[4] but even if it is not the old hands who came out with the regiment at first will have the first chance which is certainly fair as they have been nearly a year and a half from home   They cannot keep us any longer then three years from the time the regiment was mustered in as the term is for three years or sooner discharged[5]   The doller and postage stamps came safe   the dollar will do me intill we get paid   we will be mustered in for four months pay next saturday   If you have any mony that you dont think you will want to use you had better put it in a savings Bank   you will see plenty of their advertisements in the papers put it in one that is secured by real estate if you can   I will write to mother very soon and send it to you and you can send it home for me   i am sory that she is keeping the place for me for it may cause her a great deal of trouble and care and i do not intend ever to go there to stay   i am fighting for this country now and if i get through it which i expect to with Gods blessing i mean to have some benifit of it if there is any to be had   Give my love to all our friends Good by and God bless and protect you

your loving husband
PETER WELSH

1. Although this withdrawal of the New York regiments from the brigade never took place, nearly two weeks after this letter the Boston *Pilot* was still reporting that the withdrawal of these units from active service was likely to occur. Boston *Pilot*, March 7, 1863.

2. The only chaplain still with the brigade by February of 1863 was Fr. Corby with the 88th New York.

3. The "Fathers of 59th St." is probably a reference to the Paulists, whose church (St. Paul's) is located between 59th and 60th St. on Columbus Ave. in Manhattan.

4. One of the first actions taken by Joseph Hooker upon becoming commander of the Army of the Potomac was to modify General Orders No. 61, War Department, 1862, regarding leaves of absence in the field. To reduce the incentives for desertion and to improve the army's morale, Hooker's General Orders No. 3, of January 30, 1863, allowed ten-day furloughs to not more than two out of every one hundred enlisted men present for duty in a regiment. The leaves were "not to be granted

to any men but those having the most excellent record for attention to all duties." *OR*, ser. I, vol. 25, pt. 2, pp. 10–12.

5. On July 21, 1862 Governor Andrew asked for and got permission from Secretary of War Stanton to declare that men who enlisted in the old regiments from Massachusetts would be mustered out with their regiments. *OR*, series III, vol. 2, p. 240. This order was part of Andrew's continuing efforts to keep up the strength of old regiments rather than allowing their numbers to dwindle while new units were being created. The order, promulgated as General Order No. 28, was in effect from July 21 to December 31, 1862. *Mass. Adj.-Gen.* (1865), pp. 50–51.

In Camp near Falmouth   March the 8th/63

My dear wife

I received your welcome letter of the 1st to day   I am very sorry to hear that you are so lonesome and down hearted and that you have that pain in your breast   you must go to a Doctor and try to get something to do you good   it will never do to let it run   you must not think of sitting down to sew   it would destroy your health to be so confined and i do not want you to go live out   you would not like it i know   it would come very hard to you who never have been used to it and i do not want you to be nocked about among strangers   you can live well enough without going to live out or sitting down to sew constant   my pay will support you along with what you have untill i get home which will be before long i hope and if it should be long before this war is ended i will have more pay then i get now   so do not be uneasy as long as you have enough to keep you comfortable   If you had something to do that would take up a part of your time you would not feel so lonesome   but to be bound to obey the comands and whims of such people as you might chance to get a place with is something i would not wish   but when the fine weather comes if you could get a chance to go into the country in some good place for six or eight weeks it might do your health good but do not think of doing so for any longer time My dear wife you are under a mistake about the banks   a savings bank that is secured by real estate canot fail   it is not the same as banks of isue which isue bank bills   they isue more bills then the amount of their capital and lend mony to insecure partys to mak large interest and often loose the whole   and when the holders of bills get an idea that the bank is not safe they rush in with their bills an down goes the bank   but it is not so with savings banks they isue no bills and are responsible for nothing but the deposits made in the bank so that if you have a few dollars at any time that you dont want to use right away it would be the best thing you could do with it to put it in a savings bank and you can draw it out any time you want it   and it does not make any difference if goverment bills do go down or even if the goverment should be defeated in this war   real estate in New York will still be of as much value as it was before the war and such banks will have to pay the amount of their deposits in legal curency   We see the papers here regular and have all along except a few days when there was some trouble with the paper cariers   i seen in the heareld all about the conscripts law[1]   i am very glad it has passed   it will bring the people to their senses and the war will either be settled or the skulking blowers at home will have to come out and do their share of the fighting   My dear wife i wrote a letter home on last sunday and directed it to you to send it on for me   i will write to you again in a few days   do not be so long without writing to me   it is two weeks since i got a letter before this   give my love to all our friends   I must now conclude by praying God to bless and protect you

your affectionate husband
PETER WELSH

1. The conscription law, "An Act for Enrolling and Calling Out the National Forces, and for other purposes," was signed by Lincoln on March 3, 1863, although the New York *Herald* had announced its passage the previous day and published its complete text. *OR*, ser. III, vol. 3, pp. 88–93; New York *Herald*, March 2, 1863.

In Camp near Falmouth   March the 19th/63

My dear wife

I received your welcome letter of the 12th on yesterday   i am very glad to hear that you are getting better health   my health is good thank God except a slight cold which i have had for a few days   i never remember to have spent a winter and caught so little cold as i have this winter   I sleep very warm and comfortable at night   we have a door to our house and in mild weather it is almost to warm   We get plenty of soap   we cannot use half of it   we also have good socks   each man got two pair of new socks a few days ago   I have not seen any beads here   We get plenty of shugar for our coff and plenty of rations since we been in camp here   we canot eat all we got   We had a great time here on St Patricks day the whole event got up by General Meagher   there was horse race-ing and foot raceing of all kinds   nearly all the Generals in this army were present and some ladies from New York   we all got two gills of whisky each   you will see a full acount of it in the papers[1] the amusement was cut short in the evening by an order to fall in without a moments delay   the brigade was in line in light march-ing order in five minutes and ready to march   the cause of the order was that there was some skirmishing on our right about seven or eight miles up the river   we did not have to leave our camp and the boys enjoyed themselves the remainder of the evening pretty well   our army took some four or five hundred prisoners up there that day and we hear canonading today[2]   i heard that a large num-ber of our army moved up that direction yesterday   i think there will be something done here very soon from the appearence of things   i do not think that this brigade will move very soon   it is thought that we will remain here to do picket duty   I must tell you now that i have the honor of carying the green flag   when we were ordered to fall into line on St Patricks day the color bearer did not bring out the flag   when we got in line our Captain asked where the colors were and no on could tell him   our com-pany is now the color company so he told me to go and get the colors and bring them   i went to Colonels tent and got the green flag and brought it out and he made the sergeant that used to cary the flag take off the flag belt and give it to me   i put it on and the Captain told me to keep that flag and cary it   so yesterday he seen the Colnel about it and i was made color bearer   I shall feel proud to bear up that flag of green the emblem of Ireland and Irish men and espesialy having received it on that day dear to every irish heart the festivel of St Patrick   I seen James Burns on tuesday   he is well   i did not ask him if he got paid yet nor i did not inquire if he expected to get promoted but i think he will be likely to   I have to write this with a very bad pen   i think it will bother you to read some of it   we did not get paid yet but i hope we will very soon   I must now conclude praying God to bless and protect you

Your affectionate husband
PETER WELSH

1. An account of the St. Patrick's Day celebration in the Irish Brigade was carried in the Boston *Pilot* on April 4, 1863.

2. Welsh overestimates the Union success at the battle of Kelly's Ford, which took place on March 17, 1863. On that date 2100 Union cavalry under Gen. William Woods Averell engaged 800 southerners under the command of Gen. Fitz Lee. Averell's men pulled back after a full day of fighting had gained them only two miles of ground and inflicted only 133 casualties on the enemy. Averell's men suffered 78 casualties. Boatner, *Dictionary*, p. 451.

In camp near Falmouth   March the 31st/63

My dear wife

I received your welcome letter of the 26th last night   You did not mention how you were getting your health   do not neglect to let me know in your next   I am nearly well of my cold   it is a general complaint here amongst the men and some have been so bad with it that they had to go to hospital   I got the two fifty cent stamps and the three cent stamps and pens all safe   i may need the dollar if the paymaster dont come very soon   we heard that he was to be here day after tomorow   My dear wife i am sory that you feel so uneasy about my carrying the flag but it is not so bad as you think as you will see when i explain it to you   each company has to take position in line acording to the rank of captains   and by the resignation of the senior captain our companys position is the color company which is third in rank   now supposing the colors to be a dangers position i should be near them whether i carried them or not   and if as you think the colors were aimed at by the enemy i would be in full more danger in any other part of the company then carrying the flag   there is no such thing as taking shure aim in the battle field   the smoke of powder the noise of firearms and cannon and the excittement of the battle field makes it impossible   so that if the colors are fired at those on either side of the colors for the lenght of a company are more likely to get struck then the color bearer   I will give you some facts to show whether the colors are a much more dangers position then any other or not   This regiment has been in seven battles and has had but one color bearer killed and that was in the first battle in James Island[1]   he carried the national flag   in all the seven battles there was but two men wounded carrying the green flag   the sergeant who caried the national flag at fredericksburg got slightly wounded but the one that carried the green flag did not get a scratch and he was promoted leutenent next day by General Meagher   he resighned since and is now home clear of soldiering[2]   Another thing that will show you that it makes no difference what part of the regiment a man is in is that the company which carried the colors in nearly all the battles did not lose as many in killed and wounded as some other companys   and the company that carried the colors at Fredericksburg did not have as many killed and wounded as our company which was not near them   In the seven battles this regiment has been in there was but forty nine killed but there was a large number wounded[3] more men have died from sickness then have been killed since the regiment came out and this is considered one of the healthiest regiments in the field   I did not lose my comfortable little house by being made color bearer   i am still in it and attend to the drawing of rations   there is no one else in the company who understands it   they do not know how to figure up the amount a given number of men should draw   so i keep an acount and see that we get the proper alowence and the other sergeants help give it out   you would not think me unlucky if you were here this morning when a detail of about 80 men and oficers had to go out on picket   we had a snow storm last night and it turned to rain and sleet this morning   they have to go about three miles through slush and mud and stay there untill tomorow at ten Oclock when they will have to trug back again   if i was not color bearer i would have to take my turn on picket and guard now as there has been promotions in the company which would have changed me from my old job but getting the colors just saved me from it   i am not required to do any duty only go out withe colors which is only on dress parade reviews or batalion drill   i do not have to keep a musket nor cary any amunition   nothing but my knabsack grub bag and canteen   that will make it much easier for me when marching   If this brigade should be kept in front it can not do anything but skirmishing for it is to small   and in that case i will be out of it for when a regiment or brigade go out skirmishing the colors always remain behind with a reserve   You ask if there is any way that i could get clear of carrying the flag   i cannot think that you would advise me to do a mean or cowardly action   to refuse taking it when offered to me would been playing the coward   and to try to get rid of carying it now would be mean base and cowardly and i would consider it the more so on account of it being the green flag of old Irland   i will carry it as long as God gives me strenght for i know that he can as easly protect me there as if i was in the strongest tower that ever was built by the hands of man   God bless and protect you

your loving husband
PETER WELSH

1. Sgt. John J. McDonald of Co. K was the color bearer killed at James Island, June 16, 1862. McDonald was a 27-year-old merchant when he enlisted in the 28th on October 27, 1861. *Mass. Soldiers*, III 263.

2. Michael Campbell was the only sergeant of the 28th Massachusetts promoted to second lieutenant the day after Fredericksburg who had resigned by March 31, 1863, the date of this letter. Campbell was a laborer from Brookline who was mustered into the 28th on December 13, 1861 as a private. After being promoted to the commissioned ranks he resigned and was discharged on February 13, 1863. *Mass. Volunteers*, II 552; *Mass. Soldiers*, III 209.

3. Welsh greatly underestimates the number of battle deaths the 28th had suffered up to this point in the war. William F. Fox, the best authority on regimental losses, put the number of those killed and mortally wounded as of this date at 130. Fox, *Regimental Losses*, p. 169.

In camp near Falmouth   April the 10th/63

My dear wife

I received your welcome letter last night   i am very sorry to hear that your health is so bad   you should have gone to a doctor before you got so bad   and now that you have gone be shure to folow his directions and take the medecine he prescribes acording to directions for it is no use to go to a doctor if you do not folow his advice you know your health has been bad for a long time and it will take a regular course of medecine to regulate your sistem   i do not believe that you are in consumtion   doctors are often mistaken about ones disease   i know your stomac has been out of order for a long time and a disordered stomac is the source of nearly all the sickness with which we are afflicted   There is two things nesesary for your health   one is to try all in your power to keep up your spirits and not to be fretting and worrying the way you have been   and the other is to take all the out door exercise you possibly can   housing oneself up in a close room constantly is equal to taking slow poison My dear wife do not neglect to use all the means in your power to restore your health for good health is the greatest temporal blessing we have in this world   I hope with Gods blessing you will be better by the time this reaches you   I have got over my cold and i am in excelant health thank God   We had a pretty dull easter sunday here   it was stormy   i [It] snowed on saturday night and rained sunday morning so that our camp ground was all in a sluge but we have beautiful weather now   we had our eggs sunday and i had mine fried   i did not have ham but i had some very good pork to fry them with   our captain bought ten dozen for us from the sutler and as our company is small now that made a good mess for us   the sutlers charge sixty cents a dozen for eggs here and seventy five cents per pound for butter   i have tasted butter but twice since last October   i never think of such nicetys now   We had a grand review of the whole army on last wensday[1]   old Abe[2] was here   he looks as if he would soon go to kingdomcome and there is few in this army who would be sorry if he was there   there is not in the ranks of this army a more miserable looking man than old Abe   the paymaster would meet with a much heartyer welcome then he did and his visit would be much more benifecal to all concerned   I have nothing that is of much interest to write to you at present   i will write to you again soon but you need not wait for my next before you answer this for i am uneasy to hear from you to know how your health is   so be shure to answer this as soon as you receive it Give my love to all our friends   I must now conclude by praying God may bless and protect you

Your affectionate husband
PETER WELSH

1. April 8.

2. President Lincoln visited General Hooker and reviewed the Army of the Potomac in early April. It is interesting to contrast the observations of Welsh with those of another onlooker, St. Clair A. Mulholland, lieutenant colonel of the 116th Pennsylvania. While Welsh thought Lincoln "miserable looking," "as if he would soon go to kingdom come," Mulholland wrote that he wore an "air of thoughtful sadness" and that "he appeared like a man overshadowed by some deep sorrow." Of course Mulholland was writing many years after the war and may have revised his own war-time observations so as not to offend the memory of the martyred Lincoln. Mulholland, *116th Pennsylvania*, pp. 83–84.

In camp near Falmouth   April the 15th/63

My dear wife

I wrote you a letter on the tenth in answer to your last   I hope my dear wife that your health is better   i am well thank God   We are about to move at last but where we are going i dont know   we are all packed up and ready   we have to take eight days rations with us   all our clothing that we dont realy need is packed up and sent away so that we wont have two much to carry   The most of the men of this brigade are gone on piket to day so i think we will be on the reserve and have nothing more then piket duty to do   at all events nearly all the army here have moved ahead of us   we know they are moving but where or what the movement is we dont know there is no certtainty but we may remain here a week or two weeks yet   I have not much to write at present   i will write to you every time i have a chance   God bless and protect you

your affectionate husband
PETER WELSH

In camp near Falmouth   April the 20th/63

My dear wife

I received your welcome letter of the thirteenth on the sixteenth i am sory to hear that you have been so sick but i hope with the help of God that you are better.   I sent you a letter on the fifteenth in which i informed you of our being all packed up and ready to move but we are still here and no imediate sighns of moving   but we may move at any moment   that is why i did not answer your last letter sooner   i waited to see if there would be any fresh orders and also if the pay master would come but he has not   nearly all the troops around here are paid off except our division   i hope we will get paid before we leave here   I sent a certificate to Boston My Captain wrote it stating that i was here and what time i enlisted   but i could not sent any proof that i lived in Boston as there is no one in the regiment who knew me in boston   and it would be no use for me to write myself stating that i lived there as my own assertion would not be taken as proof   but i do not see why they should want any proof that i lived there as you were there and they gave the aid to you and have gave it ever since   the certificate that i am here with my description and the time i enlisted ought to be suffeciant   James Burns is well   he has got a good job he has got charge of the ambulance core of this brigade[1] so that he will be clear of fighting if we should get in to any   I must conclude now but i will write to you frequently   good by and may God bless and protect you

Your loving husband
PETER WELSH

1. At the front a second lieutenant always commanded the ambulances of a brigade, though they traveled with all the ambulances of their division, which were commanded by a first lieutenant. The division's ambulances were attended by a surgeon, an assistant surgeon, a hospital steward, a cook, and three or more nurses. Each ambulance was assigned a driver and two stretcher bearers, and a mounted sergeant accompanied every three ambulances. Lord, *They Fought for the Union,* p. 100.

In camp near Falmouth   April 26th/63

My dear wife

I sent you a letter on the twentieth   i got your last on the sixteenth   i had sent one to you the day before   We got paid up to
the first of march and i sent you $30 thirty dollars by the same way i
sent you the other mony   the regiment was paid four months pay
but the months advance that i got when i enlisted was stopeded
from me to square up the last year so that left me only thirtynine
dollars   i gave one to the Priest[1] and kept the rest for i may want a
few dollars before we get paid again   They took care to pay us just
before the regiment was mustered in for two months more pay   if
they had left it a few days longer we would had six months pay to
get   let me know in your next how you are off for mony and if you
heard anything more about the State aid   i sent a certificate and i
think it will be all right   We are still here and no more sighns of
moving then there was a week ago   My dear wife write to me
oftener   i am very uneasy about your health   i hope you are better
may God bless and protect you

Your loving husband
PETER WELSH

1. Rev. William Corby, C.S.C.

Near Scotts Mill Va   May the 2nd/63

My dear wife

I received your welcome of [sic] letter of the 23d on the evening of the 29th   i would have answered it before but i had no chance to send a letter   We left our old camp on the 29th   we have been doing picket since except while marching   we are on piket here all our brigade is here except the 88th   it is up near the front guarding amunition wagons   we have a good position here and i do not expect any rebs will trouble us if we get no nearer the enemy then we have been since we came across the river   we will be safe enough and do not expect to have anything but picket duty to do we crossed the rapahanock at U S ford on the day before yesterday the enemy offered no opesition to our army crossing   there was some fighting yesterday in front and our artilery kept up shelling all day   they are throwing a few shells to day but there is no responce from the enemy   there is a strong force of our army in front of us we are not nearer then three miles of the front lines   the place we crossed the river is about ten miles above Fredericksburg   I think old joe[1] will give the rebs more then they want this time   My dear wife i mus stop   the man who caries the mail is just going

God bless you

PETER WELSH

---

1. Joseph Hooker (1814–1879) commanded the Army of the Potomac from January 26 to June 28, 1863 when he was relieved at his own request. Nicknamed "Fighting Joe," a sobriquet he deplored, Hooker had all the qualities of a great commander. Educated at West Point (1837), decorated for gallantry in the Mexican War, and promoted for daring and skill in the Peninsula Campaign of 1862, he demonstrated leadership that justified the enthusiasm of the soldiers of the Army of the Potomac. His uncharacteristic inactivity at a critical moment at Chancellorsville, however, resulted in still another defeat at Lee's hands for the Army of the Potomac and ended Hooker's brief tenure as army commander. *DAB*.

In camp near Falmouth   May 7th/63

My dear wife

I received your last letter on the 29th of last month   i sent you a letter on the 2nd but i did not have time to write much as the man that caried the mail was going off so i had to cut it short   As you may see from the date of this letter we are back in our old camp again   we had another grand scadadle after our army driving the enemy out of Fredericksburg heming him in on the right where we were   by some mismanagement our left was broken and our army compelled to fall back[1]   we did not expect to have to go to the front from where we were on picket but we had to go up on sunday morning to support a battery and in a hot place to   we did not have to do any fiting but the shelling was terific   our brigade brought in a battery by hand of [off] the field   the horses were all killed and what men belong to it that were not killed or wounded run and left it   you will see an acount of it in the papers[2]   we were under arms saturday sunday and monday and tuesday night till two Oclock when we retreated   we fell back sunday after the battery was brought in about half a mile and built a breast work all along our line   in a few hours there was miles of breast work built   we were in the edge of a wood where we had plenty of timber and brush and we dug a trench inside in which could lay when the enemy was shelling   we had a good position and could lay behind our works and laugh at all the shell they could throw at us   they tried it but found it was only waste of powder   they then tried with infantry but fell back very quick when they felt the strenght of our position we could of held that position against any force they could bring against us but they broke the line on the left where the sixth army core was stationed   that was near the river which gave them a chance to cut us off from the ford so we had to retreat and come back to the old grong [ground] again   there was a severe thunder storm on tuesday evening   it rained terible   it ceased a little about the time we started but comenced again and raind nearly all day yesterday   the roads were in an awfull state   the mud was nearly knee deep and what was worse the most of the men had nothing to eat   the wagons had to be sent back across the river so we had to trug it through hunger wet and mud untill we got three or four miles this side of the river where we got bread   i was lucky myself   i had enough with me   the rebs would be beatten on the second days fighting only for the cowardice of some of the eleventh army core who broke and ran off the field   that gave the enemy a good position from which our army had drove them   it is over now and a failure and what the next move will be i dont know but i think it wont be across the rapahanoc   thank God i came safe and well out of it   out regiment met with but little loss   we had four or five slightly wounded   the 88th was in front while we were on picket and they lost heavly   they had 40 killed and wounded[3] James Burns lucky to be with the ambulance core   he was clear of it   I did not have time to answer your questions in my last about my position   no sergeant ranks any higher then a color sergeant and it is the most honorable position an enlisted man can have   the first sargeant of a company gets more pay   they get $20 a month   other company sargeants get $17   there can be only five sargeants in a company and although i was promoted in full form as sargeant and color bearer of the regiment i do not know whether i draw the pay yet or not as there was five sergeants belong to our company but one who was disabled and away we expect to be discharged[4] we have not heard from him for some time   i will draw the pay from the date of his discharge   My dear wife i hope your health is better   i hope to hear from you soon may God bless and protect you

your loving husband
PETER WELSH

1. Although much had gone wrong with Hooker's Chancellorsville campaign before the army's left was broken, this was the event which precipitated his decision finally to abandon his plans and once again order the army withdrawn north of the Rappahannock. On May 4th, the Union left, consisting of Gen. John Sedgwick's Sixth Corps, was attacked on three sides by the bulk of the Confederate forces while Hooker, who had an overwhelming numerical superiority over the Confederate forces that faced him on the Union right, remained inactive. During

the night of the 4th Sedgwick crossed the river with his beleaguered corps, and on the 5th the rest of the Army of the Potomac followed. Catton, *Army of the Potomac*, II 204–208.

2. Accounts of the Irish Brigade's dramatic rescue of the 5th Maine Battery on May 3, 1863 ran in the New York *Herald* on May 16th and in the Boston *Pilot* on May 30th.

3. Fox gives the 88th's losses at Chancellorsville as 3 killed and 23 wounded, although another 20 were listed as captured or missing. Fox, *Regimental Losses*, p. 217.

4. 1st Sgt. David T. Powers of Co. K never returned from his stay at David's Island Hospital in New York Harbor. He was finally dropped from the 28th's rolls as a deserter on September 1, 1863. *Mass. Soldiers,* III 265.

In camp near Falmouth   May the 10th/63

My dear wife

I received your welcome letter of April the 29th on the eight   i sent you a letter on the seventh in which i gave you some acount of our crossing the river and fighting   from later acounts of the whole afair i believe we have the best side of it   the rebel losses are very heavy   our cavelry have destroyed a great part of the railroad and bridges by which they got their supplies   My dear wife i am very glad to hear that your health is so much better   God grant that your health may be fully restored   i am in excelant health thank God although our last move was a pretty hard one i feel none the worse of it   we have beautiful weather now and we are quite comfortable here in our old camp   General Hooker very wisely isued an order before we moved that nothing should be destroyed in or about our camps   every thing to be left just as if we were here   that left us our quarters all right to come in to when we came back   he has done what i do not know of any other general doing   he had extra rations isued to all the troops who were on the battlefield who lost any as a great many did some by losing their knabsacks as they had to take them of [off] before going in to action and thousands did not have a chance to get them again   there was a great many got their rations spoiled by getting them wet   he has had rations enough isued extra to more then cover all losses   this is as it should be instead of having men suffer as they often have done for want of rations after losing them on the field of battle   old fighting joe has an eye to the welfare of his army   it is given up that this army was never so well suplied with food and clothing as it has been since he took comand of it   when we started on the last move we left as much provision in our cook house after us as would suply our company for a week after taking all we could cary   Tell James Gleason and Ann that i wish them much joy with their young daughter   i hope the mother and child are both doing well   Gods blessing be with them   let me know in your next how my little god daughter[1] is getting along and Kathy[2]   let me know also how your uncle John[3] is doing and James and his mother[4]   I forgot to state in my last that i got the dollar you sent me and the postage stamps in your last all safe   And now my dear wife i have not much more to write

this time   do not be uneasy or fretting about me   God is my pro-
tecter and in him i will put my trust   he can protect me no matter
how great the danger   May God bless and protect you

Your loving husband
PETER WELSH

1. The infant daughter of James and Ann Gleason was the godchild
of Peter Welsh.

2. Cannot identify.

3. This is probably another reference to Margaret's father's brother,
John Prendergast.

4. Cannot identify.

In camp near Falmouth   May the 13th/63

My dear wife

I seen James Burns this morning   he called here   he is going home on furlow   he is to go tomorrow morning   i thought i
would send a few lines by him   i wish i could get a furlow home
but there is no chance   there has been but five enlisted men got
furlows out of this regiment as yet and there is but little prospect
of any more   it is the fault of our Colnel   he dont want to give any
furlows   he is not proving to be so good an officer for the regiment
as he appeard to be at first   he has done a very mean action of late
which has caused a great deal of trouble among the officers and will
cause a goodeal more   instead of promoting men of his own regiment to be leutenents to fill vacancies he has got sergants and privates out of other Mass regiments and brought them into this
regiment   there is three of them here and it is said there is two
more to come[1]   this is the meanest act i have heard of any comanding officer doing in this army and especialy as his motives are purely
selfish   there was an act passed last winter autherising the war department to consolidate all the regiments whose rank and file was
reduced below half the standard for a full regiment[2]   there has
been a great many discharged from this regiment last winter who
were at hospital which brought our number down to nearly half
and if there was a few promoted and a few lost by death or discharge
the regiment would be consolidated into a batallion of four or six
companys   and the Colonel would lose comand of it as the law
provides that such batallions shall be comanded by no higher officer
then a major[3]   so in order to keep his own fat birth he has done a
great injustice to the men a great many of whom are much more
competent to hold comisions then the strangers he brought in   all
the officers of the regiment protested against it when they heard
of it and he put two captains under arest   one of them is our captain who is a gentleman in every way and a brave soldier   those
two were the leaders of the oppisition to his scheme so he tried to
wreak his wrath on them   he had them court marshaled but made
nothing of it[4]   at the time we were leaving camp to cross the rapahanock he released them from arest to take comand of their companies   and when they came to take comand we gave them three

rousing cheers and that mad him so mad that he ordered them under arest again and they have not been released yet   there is a good many of our officers resighning and i think the most of the old officers will resighn if the Colonel remains in comand[5]   but it is reported now that our number is reduced so low that our regiment will be consolidated into six companys   in that case his sheme was all in vain and we will get clear of him   My dear wife i received your last letter on the 8th and i sent you one on the tenth   i hope you are getting better health   it was a great relief to me when i read in your last letter that you were so much better   i am in good health thank God   James Burns will be able to tell you all about camp life and how we get along here   There is no sighn of our moving at present but we cant tell how soon it may be   there is one thing i wish you to do   i canot carry writing paper with me when marching without getting it spoiled and if you would enclose a sheat of small paper and an envlope in your letter when you write i would always have paper to write   there is seldom any cance to buy any when we are moving   Give my love to all our friends

Your loving husband

PETER WELSH

1. On April 6, 1863, five new second lieutenants received commissions in the 28th: William F. Cochrane, Walter S. Bailey, Theophilus F. Page, John B. Noyes, and J. Howard Tannant. All four of the new lieutenants who were actually mustered into the 28th (Tannant was never mustered) had come from other Massachusetts regiments: Cochrane came from the 1st infantry, Bailey and Page from the 2nd infantry, and Noyes from the 13th infantry. *Mass. Volunteers*, II 552; *Mass. Soldiers*, III 193, 237, 239, 250.

2. The same enrollment act of March 3, 1863 that called for conscription of able-bodied men between the ages of 20 and 45 also, in section 19, called for the consolidation of the companies of any regiment whose strength fell below half of the maximum number prescribed by law. *OR*, ser. III, vol. 3, p. 91.

3. Actually, according to General Orders No. 86 of the Adjutant General's Office, dated April 2, 1863, infantry regiments that had been consolidated into "five or less number of companies" had to muster out

"the colonel, the major, and one assistant surgeon." *OR*, ser. III, vol. 3, p. 112.

4. Colonel Byrnes had Capt. Charles H. Sanborn of Welsh's company (Co. K) and Capt. Jeremiah W. Coveney of Co. F brought before a General Court Martial convened at Division Headquarters on April 20, 1863. The most formidable charge lodged against them was having engaged in "mutinous and seditious conduct" while the regiment was expecting orders to march against the enemy. Two days of testimony revealed them guilty of some lesser offenses, but the court was unwilling to accept the implications of Colonel Byrnes' more serious charge of mutinous conduct. Both were sentenced to be publicly reprimanded in General Orders by the major general commanding the division. Court Martial Records, NA.

5. Since the first of the year three captains, five first lieutenants, and two second lieutenants had resigned from the 28th. *Mass. Volunteers*, II 550–53.

In camp near Falmouth   May the 27th/63

My dear wife

I received your welcome letter on the twenty fifth   i am sory to hear that your health is not improving as fast as i hoped it was but you must not be disheartened   it may still be necessary for you to take more medicine and you can not expect to feel well or strong while you are taking medicine   i hope with the blessing of God that you will soon be well   There was a very long intervel between your last two letters   the one before this i received on the eight   i sent you letters on the second seventh and tenth of this month and one hy James Burns[1]   let me know in your next if you received them all   i would have answered this one sooner but i was so busy that i did not have time   we moved our camp last friday   we are now about a mile nearer to the railroad in a very nice place   i have been busy ever since we moved fixing up our new quarters   i have got just the purtyest little shanty in this army   i built it for myself and the first sergeant[2]   i also built one for our Captain[3]   all the oficers are trying to get up ones like them but they cant come it   Our core has got the job of guarding the railroad here so that we will be likely to remain here for some time unless the capture of vicksburg[4] which you have heard of before this should caus any suden change in our movements here   however if there should be a movement here we will be the last to move as the railroad must be guarded as long as the enemy is any where near   The capture of Vicksburg is a great victory for us as it is of more importance then any other stronghold in the posession of the enemy   one well directed blow in this state now would kill the rebellion efectualy   God grant that the end of this wreched war may soon come   I would like to have a prayer book if you could get me a very small one which i could cary in my pocket conveniantly   tell James Burns that his friend a sergeant in the 69th was over here   i forget his name but it is the one i seen at his mothers last summer[5]   he expects a letter from James   tell him also that Major Smith[6] has been very sick   the doctor says that he has got the measels   i seen him night before last   he was a little better then   he expects to go home on a sick furlow   My health is excelant thank God   we have had some very hot days here but it is cooler now   It would be impossible for you to come out here   if the war is not over before the latter part of this summer i will get a chance to go home to see you   Give my love to all our friends   i will write to you again in a few days and write a letter to your father which you can send home

Gods choicest blessings be with you
your loving husband
PETER WELSH

1. The letter of May 13, 1863 must have been sent to New York with James Byrnes who was on his way home. He was mustered out of the 88th New York a month later, but he enrolled in the regiment again in April of 1864 as a first lieutenant. Phisterer, *New York in the War,* IV 2983.

2. Patrick Nolan was a wagoner from Milford, Massachusetts when he enlisted in the 28th in September 1861. He made first lieutenant and then captain before he was killed in action at Deep Bottom on August 14, 1864. *Mass. Soldiers,* III 264.

3. Captain Sanborn.

4. An erroneous dispatch of May 24, 1863 from the telegraph messenger at Memphis reported that the stars and stripes flew over Vicksburg and that victory was complete. In fact, the siege of Vicksburg was not successful until July 4, 1863. Boston *Pilot,* May 30, 1863.

5. Cannot identify.

6. This is probably a reference to Maj. John Smith of the 88th New York. When James Byrnes mustered into Co. A of the 88th in 1861 Smith had been his captain. Smith rose to the rank of major on February 5, 1863 and had actually been promoted to lieutenant colonel on May 13, 1863, before this letter was written. Phisterer, *New York in the War,* IV 2991.

PETER WELSH

Camp of the 28th Regiment Mass Vol
Near Falmouth Va   June the 1st/63

My dear sir[1]

It is under very pecular circumstances that i now adress you First never having adressed you by letter before   Secondly on acount of my present position which no doubt seems so unacountable to you   To you as the father of my dear wife i do not wonder that it should seem very very [sic] strange that i should volunteerly joine in the bloody strife of the battlefield   And to her dear mother i know it must be still more painfull   As a mothers love for her children is the most pure and enduring   Her care for their happiness and welfare is the most anxious and painfull   On Margarets acount it must seem to you all very misfortunate   Especialy when looked at from such a distance as all circumstances whether good or bad become magnified in proportion to the distance we are from them   It is but natural that you should feel so   And with regard to my present position i can very well understand your feelings   I know pretty well in what light people view soldiering in Irland   Nor do i wonder that such a feeling exists   For i consider an Irishman who volunterly enlists in the British service merits the utter contempt of his countrymen   Seven centuries of persecution Churches Convents and Monesteries plundered and destroyed Conviscated property Murdered patriots and inocent women and children slaughtered in cold blood With inumerable other barbarities of the most fiendish discription which from time to time have been comited in unfortunate Irland by that prostitute of nations that amalgamation of hipocricy base treachry and debauchry called the British Government Should rise like a mountain over the despicable Irishman who would volunterly join her service with the possibility of living by any other means and crush him into eternal oblievion   In this country it is very different Here we have a free goverment just laws and a Constitution which guarentees equal rights and privelages to all   Here thousands of the sons and daughters of Irland have come to seek a refuge from tyrany and persecution at home   And thousands still continue to come   Here they have an open field for industry   And those who posses the abilitys can raise themselves to positions of honor and

100

emolument   Here Irishmen and their decendents have a claim a stake in the nation and an interest in its prosperity   Irishmen helped to free it from the yoke of Britain and to build on this soil the best and most liberal goverment in the world   They have borne a willing and a formidable part in the subsequent wars of the country with England and Mexico   And have rushed by thousands to the call of their adopted country in the present unfortunate strugle   Their blood has stained every battlefield of this war   Thousands of Irlands brave sons lay mouldering in the soil of Virgenia Missouri Maryland and Tenesee and in every state where a battle has been fought   And should those brav lives be sacrafised in vain   The heart of every true Irishman will answer no emphaticaly no   They had a vital interest in the preservation of our national existence the perpetuation of our instutions and the free and untrameled exicution of our laws   We who survive them have a double motive then to nerve us to action   We have the same nationel political and social interests at stake not only for ourselves but for coming generations and the opressed of every nation for America was a comon asylum for all   And we have the stern fact before us that thousands of our race have sacrafised their lives in this cause and should we now fail to suport it they would have faught bled and dyed in vain   Would to God that every man in the loyel states felt truly and unselfishly how great an interest he has in the supression of this helish rebellion   No rebellion the world ever saw was so fouly ploted nor originated from such slight cause   If they could but see the great and vital conseqences that now hang between victory and defeat they would rush like an avelanch upon this cursed rebellion and sweep it from the land But in this as in all civel wars base treachery selfish interests and incompetency are playing their part   Had this been a war with any foreighn power it would have been ended in half the time The question has often been asked and not a few foolishly adhere to the idea[:] What have foreighn born citizens to do with this war they will say   The agitation of the question which brought on this war originated and was kept up by a party composed almost wholy of native born citizens   They were the cause of the war and let them fight it out   Silly argument   If you and i and a third party are joint owners of a piece of property and you and him differ about the cource to to [sic] be pursued in the management of that property he becomes exasperated and undertakes to destroy it rather than that you should manage it acording to your own conception of what was best   Am i to stand by with folded arms and see him acomplish his desighns without raising a hand in defence of my own rights   I should be false to both your interests and my own if i would   And so is the foreighn born citizen who holds himself aloof from this strugle False to his own and his felow citizens interests   for he would alow the third party to destroy his goverment and deprive himself and his fellow men of their rights and libertys   And this is especialy true of Irishmen   America is Irlands refuge Irlands last hope   destroy this republic and her hopes are blasted   If Irland is ever ever [sic] free the means to acomplish it must come from the shores of America   To the people of different nations who have emigrated here and become part of its native population Irland owes nothing   in fact they are rather her debtors   But to this country Irland owes a great deal   How many thousands have been rescued from the jaws of the poorhouse and from distress and privation by the savings of the industrious sons and more particularly by the daughters of Irland who have emigrated here   It is impossible to estimate the amount of distress and misery that has been warded off from the down troden and tyrant crushed people of many of the poorer districts of Irland by this means   Without this field for their industry those noble hearted girls could never have rendered this service to their friends But would have been a burden on them at home to crush them still deeper in distress   Irland is bound to this country by the strongest tyes of blood and simpathy   Her sons have penetrated to the remotest parts of the union   they are interwoven like a network over the whole face of the country   Their influence is felt in every section and it is increasing and will continue untill at no very distant day the Irish element will be the most powerfull and influential in the land   When we are fighting for America we are fighting in the interest of Irland striking a double blow cutting with a two edged sword   For while we strike in defence of the rights of Irishmen here we are striking a blow at Irlands enemy and opressor

England hates this country because of its growing power and greatness She hates it for its republican liberty and she hates it because Irishmen have a home and a goverment here and a voice in the counsels of the nation that is growing stronger every day which bodes no good for her England hates this country because we have out riveled her as a naval power and are fast outriveling her as a comercial power There is but one step more which a few years of peacefull progress will acomplish that is to surpass her as a manufacturing nation and Englands star of asendency will have set to rise no more Those are powerfull motives with an Englishman when you touch his pocket you awaken his worst passions And thus because England feared that America by her growing trade and comerce would draw the gold from her own coffers she has ploted for years to destroy her growing rivel It was in England that acursed agitation of the slavery question origenated Thousands of pounds have been colected yearly to carry it on the origenaters of it found willing dupes in this country to cary out their program Ambitious men and greedy politecians seised on it as a means by which to get themselves into influential and lucrative situations thus the agitation was kept up untill it shook the country to its very foundation Those are but a few of the many powerfull motives that influence Irishmen to take up arms in defense of this goverment such motives as impelled those brave sons of Irland Generels Shields[2] Muligan[3] Corcoran[4] and T F Meagher with many others talented and influential to unsheath their swords and expose themselves to all the hardships and dangers of war Such motives have influenced me with the desire that i have felt from my childhood that i might one day have an oppertunity when the right man to lead should be found and the proper time should arive to strike a blow for the rights and liberty of Irland For such an oppertunity this war is a school of instruction for Irishmen and if the day should arive within ten years after this war is ended an army can be raised in this country that will strike terror to the saxons heart It is just nine months since i joined the service i am color sergeant of my regiment i cary the green flag of Erin all the Irish regiments cary the green flag as well as the nationel flag I received the green flag on last St. Patricks day i feel proud to bear that emblem of Irlands pride and glory and it shall never kiss the dust while i have strenght to hold it   I have but one regret and that is on my dear wifes acount   she of course is lonesome and freted on my acount   She is not however in any want of means for her suport during my absence   her only trouble is about the dangers to which i am exposed but i am in no trouble on this acount I put my trust in God   i know that he can protect me here as easily as if i was in a fortified tower with no enemy to asail it   I hope this war will soon come to an end   then we will be happy together once more and i hope at no very distant day to see you all   nothing could give me greater pleasure then to go to see you and see that dear old land i love so much   And now i must draw to a close for i am short of space and had to crowd this so that i fear you can scarcely read it And now my dear father and mother sisters and brothers acept from my heart my best wishes my warmest love and cincerest prayers that God may shower his choicest blessings on you all   May all happiness both spiritual and temporal be with you   farewell

Yours cincerely

PETER WELSH

Mr Patrick Prendergast

1. This letter was addressed to Margaret's father, Patrick Prendergast, living in Ireland.

2. Born in Ireland, James Shields (1806–1879) came to the United States in 1826. Before the war he was very active in Democratic politics and served with distinction in the Mexican War as a brigadier general of Illinois volunteers. Appointed brigadier general of U. S. Volunteers in 1861, Shields campaigned in the Shenandoah Valley, winning recognition at Winchester (May 25, 1862) and Port Republic (June 9, 1862) before resigning his commission on March 28, 1863. *DAB*.

3. James A. Mulligan (1830–1864) was born in Utica, New York of Irish parents. Mulligan practiced law and edited a Roman Catholic newspaper called the *Western Tablet* before the war. During the war he was offered a commission as brigadier general of U. S. Volunteers, but he declined the promotion so he could remain in command of the Irish regiment, the 23rd Illinois, which he had raised. He was mortally

wounded at Winchester, Virginia on July 23, 1864 and died three days later in the enemy's hands. *Appletons' Cyclopaedia.*

4. Born in Ireland, Michael Corcoran (1827–1863) came to the United States in 1849. He joined the 69th New York State Militia as a private, but rose to command it before the war commenced. He led the 69th at First Bull Run, was wounded, and was captured by the Confederates. Finally exchanged in August 1862, he was commissioned brigadier general and organized the Corcoran Legion. He was killed in August 1863 when his horse fell on him while he was riding with General Meagher. *Appletons' Cyclopaedia.*

Near Fairfax station   June the 18th/63

My dear wife

I have not time to write any particulars at present   we left before fredericksburg on sunday night   i have had no chance to write to you since last saturday untill now   we were on picket reserve the whole regiment from saturday till sunday night   we have been marching ever since   we are not far from Washington now   I am well thank God   I did not receive any letter from you since i wrote last   the mails did not come   good by

God bless you
PETER

P S   I will write you a long letter as soon as i have a chance

2D IRISH REGIMENT

FAUGH A BALLAUGH

Of Massachusetts IRISH VOLUNTEEERS
By Order of GOVERNOR ANDREW.

HEAD QUARTERS AT MARBLE HALL
HOWARD STREET, NEAR THE HOWARD ATHENAEUM, BOSTON,
Where every accommodation will be afforded to Recruits who desire to enlist for the War.

THIS REGIMENT WILL BE COMMANDED BY

COL. T. S. MURPHY,

Late Commander of the New York Montgomery Guards, a gentleman qualified to command any Regiment.

100 DOLLARS BOUNTY.   Pay and Rations upon Enlistment.

The people of many of the towns and cities of the Commonwealth have made ample provision for those joining the ranks of the Army. If any person enlists in a Company or Regiment out of the Commonwealth they cannot share in the bounty which has been thus liberally voted.

The Recruits for this Regiment will go into Camp at once
at CAMP CAMERON, Cambridge, and all who desire to serve in the ranks of this Regiment should make application to _____ Deputy Recruiting Agent.

In _____ Office at _____

PATRICK DONOHOE, - - DR. W. M. WALSH.

M. H. KEENAN'S CARD AND JOB PRESS, 104 WASHINGTON STREET, BOSTON.

1861 recruiting poster for the 28th Massachusetts. The 9th Massachusetts had already been raised as the Commonwealth's 1st Regiment of Irish Volunteers, thus making the 28th the 2nd Irish Regiment.
Photo: courtesy Massachusetts Historical Society

VOLUNTEER ENLISTMENT.

STATE OF *Massachusetts*

City TOWN OF *Boston Charlestown*

I, *Peter Welch* in the State of *British Provinces*, born in *Prince Edwards Isle* aged *Thirty one* years, and by occupation a *Carpenter*, Do HEREBY ACKNOWLEDGE to have volunteered this *Third* day of *September* 18 *62*, to serve as a SOLDIER in the ARMY OF THE UNITED STATES OF AMERICA, for the period of THREE YEARS, unless sooner discharged by proper authority: Do also agree to accept such bounty, pay, rations, and clothing as are or may be established by law for volunteers. And I, *Peter Welch* do solemnly swear that I will bear true faith and allegiance to the UNITED STATES OF AMERICA, and that I will serve them honestly and faithfully against all their enemies or opposers whomsoever; and that I will observe and obey the orders of the President of the United States, and the orders of the officers appointed over me, according to the Rules and Articles of War.

Sworn and subscribed to, at *Boston* this *Third*, day of *Sept* 18 *62*, *Peter Welch* BEFORE me *John Bates, Justice of the Peace*

28th Reg't

I CERTIFY, ON HONOR, That I have carefully examined the above named Volunteer, agreeably to the General Regulations of the Army, and that in my opinion he is free from all bodily defects and mental infirmity, which would, in any way, disqualify him from performing the duties of a soldier.

Daniel H. Hand M. D.
EXAMINING SURGEON.

I CERTIFY, ON HONOR, That I have minutely inspected the Volunteer, *Peter Welch* previously to his enlistment, and that he was entirely sober when enlisted; that, to the best of my judgment and belief, he is of lawful age; and that, in accepting him as duly qualified to perform the duties of an able-bodied soldier, I have strictly observed the Regulations which govern the recruiting service. This soldier has *Hazel* eyes, *Brown* hair, *fresh* complexion, is *5* feet *8* inches high.

Capt. H. Chamberlin

11 Regiment of *Mass* Volunteers.
RECRUITING OFFICER.

Peter Welsh enlists in the 28th Massachusetts on September 3, 1862.

To all whom it may Concern.

Know ye, That _Peter Welsh_ a _Sergeant_ of Captain _James E. McIntire_ Company, (K) _28_ Regiment of _Mass. Foot Vols_ VOLUNTEERS who was enrolled on the ___ day of _August_ one thousand eight hundred and _sixty-two_, to serve _three_ years or during the war, is hereby **Discharged** from the service of the United States, this _thirty-first_ day of _December_, 1863, at _Stevensburg Virginia_ by reason of _Re-enlistment_

(No objection to his being re-enlisted is known to exist.)

Said _Peter Welsh_ was born in _Charlestown_ in the State of _Ireland_ ___ years of age, _5_ feet _8_ inches high, _light_ complexion, _Hazel_ eyes, _Brown_ hair, and by occupation, when enrolled a ___

Given at _Stevensburg_ this _Thirty-first_ day of _December_ 1863.

* This sentence will be erased should there be anything in the conduct or physical condition of the soldier rendering him unfit for the Army.

[A. G. O. No. 99.]

R. Byrnes
Col. Commanding the Reg't.

Peter Welsh is discharged on the last day of 1863 to re-enlist as a sergeant on the first day of the new year. The document misspells his name and misstates his age, occupation, and place of birth; it is signed by Col. Richard Byrnes.

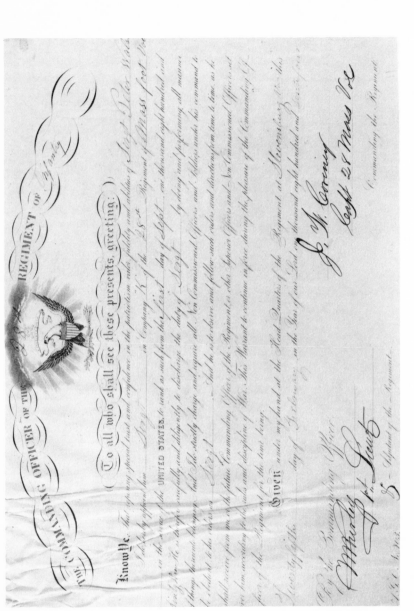

Peter Welsh's official promotion to sergeant on September 1, 1863 is confirmed on February 25, 1864. It is signed by Capt. Jeremiah W. Coveney.

Brig. Gen. Thomas Francis Meagher
in his dress uniform as commander
of the Irish Brigade.
Photo: courtesy Michael J. McAfee

Col. Richard Byrnes,
commanding officer of
the 28th Massachusetts.
Carte-de-visite photo: courtesy
U. S. Army Military History Institute,
Carlisle Barracks, Pennsylvania

Capt. Charles H. Sanborn,
commanding Co. K,
28th Massachusetts.
Carte-de-visite photo: courtesy
U. S. Army Military History Institute,
Carlisle Barracks, Pennsylvania

The Boston *Pilot* on January 18, 1862 reports the presentation
of the first green flag to the 28th Massachusetts.
Photo: courtesy Boston Public Library

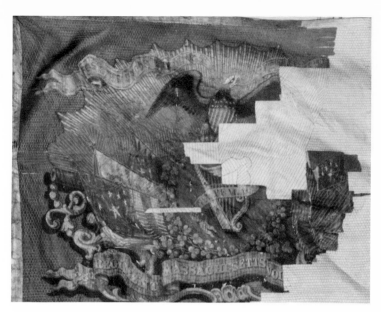

The tattered remnant of the 28th Massachusetts' first green flag,
preserved in the State House at Boston.
Photo: Collin MacDonald

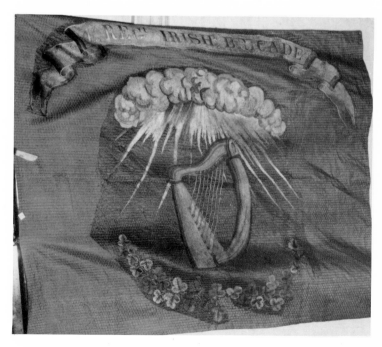

Remnants of the second or third green flag carried by the
28th Massachusetts (as 4th Regiment, Irish Brigade),
preserved in the State House at Boston. The fragments
have been mounted on a new green backing.
Photo: Collin MacDonald

The patriotic stationery to which Margaret Welsh objected.

Peter Welsh's letter of February 8, 1863, though written on even more
colorfully patriotic stationery, contains his apology for its use.
Thereafter, he will use plain paper and envelopes.

Peter Welsh hurriedly assures his wife that he has come safely out of
the "terifick battle" at Gettysburg.

Rev. William Corby, c.s.c.,
some years after the War.
Peter Welsh had frequent contact
with him after the 28th Massachusetts
joined the Irish Brigade.
*Photo: courtesy University of
Notre Dame Archives*

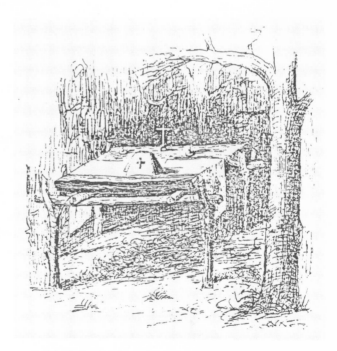

In his Christmas 1862 letter, Peter Welsh describes a rustic
altar of the type depicted in Fr. Corby's *Memoirs*.

Peter Welsh's last letter.

Carver Hospital, Washington, D.C.
Photo: courtesy NA

Margaret Welsh's telegram
to her uncle James Gleason.

FORTYSIX. WASHN MAY THIRTIETH. JAS GLEASON. TWENTYEIGHT MADISON ST NY.

1030/13   25

HL IS DEAD AND WILL BE IN WORK IN MORNING. MARGARET WELSH.

MERICAN TELEGRAPH COMPANY,
CONNECTING ALL THE CITIES AND TOWNS IN THE UNITED STATES.
Y OFFICES AT THE PRINCIPAL HOTELS.
General Office, 145 Broadway.

HARGE.

Peter Welsh's monument in Calvary Cemetery, Woodside, Queens, New York.
Photos: Lawrence Frederick Kohl

Margaret Prendergast Welsh,
in a photograph taken
probably after the War.
Carte-de-visite photo:
R. A. Lewis, 160 Chatham Street,
New York City

In Ireland in 1866, Margaret Welsh receives some of her Widow's Pension.

July the 6th/63   five miles from Gettysburg Pa

My dear wife

I have not time to write any particulars at present   i came out
of this terifick battle[1] safe and unhurt thank God   i had no chance
to send you a letter since we were near fairfax station Va   good by
and God bless you   the mail is going   i can not write any more
i did not know there would be a chance to send a letter this morning
or i would wrote more

1. The battle of Gettysburg, July 1–3, 1863. See illustration.

Pleasant Vally Maryland   July the 17th/63

My dear wife

I am happy that i have an oppertunity to write to you to day   i
have had verry little chance to write for the last month   This has
been the severest campaighn of the war   This core was the last to
leave Fredericksburg   Our brigade went on picket on saturday
evening June the 13th in a severe thunderstorm   we lay on the
bank of the Rapahanock untill dark sunday evening   we then
started and marched all night and next day untill one Oclock   the
day was very hot   we got into the woods then and lay there untill
daylight next morning   we started then and marched all day untill
dark   the day was very hot and the dust was sufficating   next
morning we started at eight Oclock and marched to a place near
fairfax station   we got there about one P M   there was hundreds
of men who had to fall out of the ranks and stay behind   the
weather was so hot and we were on a forced march   we remained
at this place two days   i wrote you a few lines there and got a
letter from you before we left   we marched at four P M on friday
and went to Centervill   remained there over night and marched
next day at noon and went to thoroughfare gap   we marched over
twenty miles that afternoon   it was midnight when we halted
the roads being very bad as it raind very heavy the night before
We went up on the mountain at the west side of the gap sunday
morning and remained on picket there four days   We evacuated
our position at nine A M on thursday and marched to a place called
pleasant vally Va   camped for the night and started early next
morning and arrived at Edwards ferry on the Potomac in the afternoon   halted about a mile from the ferry and piched tents just
at dark   got orders to strike tents and started for the ferry   there
was so many troops to cross that it was midnight when we got into
a field about a mile on this side of the river where we lay down for
the night   We started next day at four P M and marched untill
eleven at night where we threw ourselves down to sleep   started
next morning at daylight and marched to Fredericks Citty and
camped within a short distance of where i first joined the regiment
before the battle of south mountain last summer   next morning
we started at seven A M and marched to Uniontown a distance of

thirty two miles   This was the greatest march ever made by any part of our army in heavy marching order   ours was the only core that done it   the others that were en route for there all stoped befor they got there and came up next day and our core numbered very small that night when we got there at eleven Oclock   there was thousands on the road who had to lay behind unable to come up   we did not have over forty of our regiment when we halted The Major of one batallion of our brigade turned round to give orders to his men and found he had but one man to comand   i was the only man of my company that was able to cook coffe after we halted   i went over half a mile for water and had my supper before i lay down   We remained there the next day and marched the day folowing into Pencilvenia to a place within three miles of the battle ground of Gettysburg   the fighting had comenced that day at nine A M   we started next morning at five A M went to the front and formed in line of battle   there was no fighting except picket skir-mishing untill four P M when the enemy comenced the atack on our left   we were ordered in at six Oclock in a skirt of woods where the enemy was pressing our lines hard   it was at the base of a hill which he wanted to gain[1]   had he gained that hill he could easily have driven us from our position   it was a hot place   our little brigade fought like heroes and we drove the the [sic] enemy nearly a quarter of a mile when he threw a heavy force against the brigade on the right of ours driving them which let him in on our flank   by this we were compeled to fall back but luckily there was a part of another core coming to relieve us   this force drove the enemy back holding the ground   We lost heavely   the killed wounded and missing of our little regiment is over a hundred[2] Out of five regiments that form this brigade there is but men enough here present to make three full companys[3]   The most desperet fighting was on the third day   the enemy opened about one hundred and fifty pieces of artilery on our line all at wonct the hissing of shot and noise of shell was most terible   the enemy charged on our lines at at [sic] different points but was every where repulsed with frightfull loss   our was well handled   they let them burn away untill they saw the proper oppertunity and then they gave it to them with terible efect   Lee[4] got severely whiped on a

fair field at Gettysburg and by a force smaller then his own[5]   on
saturday there was no fighting except with our skirmishing driving
in the enemys pickets   on sunday our forces comenced to advance
after the enemy   our core moved back to a place called two taverns
we rested there for a day   i wrote you a few lines that morning[6]
I will give you an acount of our marching since in my next   i have
not room in this   My dear wife i am sorry to hear that your feet
are troubling you again   i did not think you would be able to
stand that work   it is to fateiguing   you must content yourself
and take all the rest you can   i know you would not feel the time
so long nor feel so lonesome if you were doing something that
would take up your attention   but it is no use for you to try to do
what you are not able to do   I am in good health thank God   i
have a great deal to be thankfull for   i have come out safe and
unhurt where thousands have been wounded and killed   I hope to
hear from you soon   I am sorry to hear that there is such disgracefull riots[7] in New York   i hope it will not get near to you
nor anoy you   i read a full acount of it in yesterdays paper   the
report was up to twelve oclock wensday night   i see they tried the
virtue of grape and canister on them and it had a very good efect
the originaters of those riots should be hung like dogs   they are
agents of jef davis[8] and had their plans laid [to] start those riots
simultanesly with Lees raid into Pensilvenia   i hope the authoru-
tys will use canister freely   it will bring the bloody cutthroats to
their censes   I must stop for want of room   i will write again soon
God bless and protect you

> your loving husband
> PETER WELSH

1. Little Round Top.

2. The *Official Records* give the 28th's losses as 8 killed, 57 wounded,
and 35 captured or missing for a total of 100 casualties. *OR*, ser. I, vol.
27, pt. 1, p. 175. But Conyngham put the 28th's casualties at 107 out
of the 224 engaged. Conyngham, *Irish Brigade*, p. 578.

3. Col. Patrick Kelly, who led the Irish Brigade at Gettysburg, reported 202 casualties out of the 530 men the brigade took into action.
OR, ser. I, vol. 27, pt. 1, p. 386.

4. The greatest of southern commanders, Robert E. Lee (1807–1870) had "qualities of intellect and character that made him a legend in his own lifetime." His brilliant leadership of the Army of Northern Virginia (1862–1865) frustrated the Army of the Potomac and kept the South in the war far longer than their manpower and resources should have allowed. Lee graduated second in his class at West Point (1829), won a brilliant reputation in the Mexican War, and acted as Superintendant at West Point before the war. Offered the command of the Federal armies by Lincoln, Lee chose to follow his home state of Virginia into the Confederacy. *DAB*.

5. Welsh is mistaken when he asserts that the Union forces were outnumbered at Gettysburg. Livermore puts the effectives at Gettysburg at 83,289 Federals and 75,054 Confederates. *Numbers & Losses*, pp. 102–103.

6. See letter of July 6, 1863.

7. From Monday, July 13 until Thursday, July 16, 1863, New York City was torn by terrible rioting, which the institution of the draft had precipitated. The violence, aimed first at the draft office and the Second Avenue Armory, was eventually turned against the black population. The mobs, made up largely of immigrant Irish workingmen, saw blacks not only as the cause of the war, but also as competitors for jobs in the New York labor market. Troops fresh from the battle at Gettysburg had to be called in to quell the rioting. In four days the rioting had snuffed out hundreds of lives and caused millions of dollars of property damage. Allan Nevins, *The War for the Union*, III: *The Organized War, 1863–1864* (New York: Scribners, 1971), 119–25.

8. Jefferson Davis (1808–1889) was the only president the Confederate States of America had during its brief existence. Kentucky-born and West Point–educated (1828), Davis was a Mississippi planter before serving in the U. S. House (1845–46), the Senate (1847–51, 1857–61), and as Secretary of War under Franklin Pierce (1853–57). *DAB*.

Bloomfield Va   July the 22nd/63

My dear wife

I wrote you a letter on the 17th and i received a letter from you on the same evening   i gave you an acount in my last of our marching up to our arrivel at two taverns Pa   After resting there a day we marched to tanyes town Md[1] camped there over night and next morning it was raining very heavy   we struck tents and marched for Fredericks Citty   this was the hardest march we have had   the rain fell in torrents all the forenoon   the road was almost knee deep with mud and water   we marched twenty two miles that day and camped within five miles of Fredericks Citty Marched at five A M next morning passed through the citty and went to cramtons gap   camped for the night   Marched at five next morning crossed Antetam creek and advanced to the enemys pickets formed a line of battle and remained there all night   Moved at seven next morning and advanced to Jones cross roads where our cavelry were skermishing with the enemy   we formed our line here and lay in position untill two P M the next day when we advanced our line about a mile   we had a severe thunder storm that evening   that was sunday the 12th   our troops threw up a line of earthworks that night   we remained there monday and made a general advance at eight A M   tuesday morning advanced to Williamsport but the enemy had all left   we then changed our course down the river   our Cavelry were skermishing with the enemy untill they cut of [off] their retreat at falling waters where they captured about two thousand of them[2]   We lay there all night and marched wensday morning for Harpers ferry   we camped beside the river that night within two miles of the fery   next morning we moved into Pleasent Vally where we remained until five A M saturday morning when we crossed the Potomac at Harpers ferry and came about five miles and camped   struck tents at eleven A M on sunday and marched about ten miles   camped   marched next morning and camped here monday evening   It is reported that we are going to Warenton but i do not know where we may form our next base of operations   I see by your last letter that it was reported in New York that we were defeated in Pencilvenia   nothing could be more false   when i wrote you them few lines at two taverns i did not have time to write any particulars as the man who caried the letters was going away before i knew there was any chance to send one   nor did i think it necessary to mention that we had beaten Lee for i did not think that the most black hearted traitor would dare to invent a report that we were defeated where our victory was so complete   i know how that battle wound up for i saw with my own eyes   on the third day our army drove lees right about three miles   i seen the enemy atack our lines at two different points that day and they were mowed down like grass before the sythe while advancing and when they came close upon our line our forces advanced upon them completely skattering them and capturing thousands[3]   They left their dead and wounded on the field   this i know to be a fact for our own men buried their dead and our ambulance corps took their wounded off the field the ambulance wagons blong to our division was steadily at work for thirty hours carrying the rebel wounded off the field   I seen the last outpost of the enemys picket driven in by our skirmishers and seen with my own eyes on the morning of the fifth our army advancing following up the enemy for our core was the last to leave the field   after the advance was made our core and the twelfth came back to Maryland the same way we went   Gettysburg was the most decided defeat Lee ever met with   even the disafected of New York will have to acknoledge that the union army is doing something for the Capture of Vicksburg is no longer a rumer but a fact as is the surender of Port Hudson[4] also   A pretty time they are getting up mob riots when one unanimous efort might finish up this acursed war in a few weeks   jeffs agents have been working very slyly and cuning but they will be foiled in all their skemes every leader and instigator of those riots should be made an example of   there was hundreds no doubt mixed into them that did not know what they were doing caried away by excitement and under the influence of traitorous cut throats who made them believe they were resisting a great wrong   they could not labour under a more false impression   no conscription could be fairer then the one which is about to be enforced   it would be impossible to frame it to satisfy every one   And those drafted men may never have to fight a battle   the sucessfull carrying out of this draft will do more

to end the war then the wining of a great victory   it will show the
south that we have the determination and the power to prosecute
the war and they have no possible means of raising an adiquate
force to oppose the army we can raise by this conscription   thus
they must soon see the hopelessness of their cause   and they are
not fools nor madmen enough to continue the prosecution of a
war that is wasting their resources destroying their homes property
and people without a reasonable prospect of sucess   My dear wife
i am troubled a goodeal about you   i can see from your letters
that you are teribly fretted   do try and be more reconciled to the
circumstances in which we are placed   trust in God   he is good
and mercifull   you are wearing yourself away and destroying your
health by this constant fretting and worrying   be of good cheer
my dear wife   we will be happy together yet with the blessing of
God   I am in excelant health thank God   in fact i am quite a
different man from what i was altogether   i do not know what it
is to feel sick now   give my love to all our friends

Your loving husband
PETER WELSH

1. Taneytown, Maryland.

2. On July 14, 1863, Union cavalry under Gens. John Buford and
Judson Kilpatrick fell on Lee's rear guard under Gens. Henry Heth
and William D. Pender near Falling Waters on the Potomac. Although
erroneous reports of the capture of 2,000 Confederates were published
in the newspapers, the Union cavalry actually captured only 719 officers
and men before the commands of Heth and Pender were able to cross the
river into West Virginia. Edwin B. Coddington, *The Gettysburg Campaign: A Study in Command* (New York: Scribners, 1968), pp. 570–72.

3. Most authorities put the number of Confederates captured and
missing for July 1–3 at slightly more than 5,000. Boatner, *Dictionary*,
p. 339.

4. Port Hudson, Louisiana, the last Confederate strong point on the
Mississippi River, fell on July 8, 1863. Gen. Frank Gardner's force of
almost 6,000 surrendered to Gen. Nathaniel Banks, whose Army of the
Gulf had been besieging the garrison since the end of May. Long, *Civil
War Day by Day*, p. 381.

In camp near Kellys ford   August 2nd/63

My dear wife

I have not received any letter from you since the 17th of last month   i sent you a letter that morning   we were then at Bloomfield   i received one from you on that evening   i wrote you one right away but did not have a chance to send it for several days   we do not have regular mail comunication so you must not feel uneasy if you do not hear from me regular   We have not had very hard marching since i last wrote   we were at Manasses gap   we arived there on the night of the same day that the third army corps had a skirmish with the enemy but they skidadeled that night and we left there next day   We arived here day before yesterday   the weather is very hot   we are encamped in the woods here where we have good shade   I do not think we will have any more fighting for some time   there will be some changes in this army and the drafted men are to be brought out   there has been Officers and men sent out of all the Mass regiments to bring them out[1]   My dear wife i hope you are getting better health and i also hope that you are in better spirits   i enjoy excelant health thank God   I hope that disturbance is all put down in New York   i hope it did not come near enough to you to anoy you   I am very sorry that the Irish men of New York took so large a part in them disgracefull riots   God help the Irish   They are to easily led into such snares which gives their enemys an oppertunity to malighn and abuse them   I have not much news to write you at presen   Give my love to all our friends   May God bless an protect you

your loving husband
PETER WELSH

1. Although the quality of draftees might have been low, their chief sin was often only their poverty. But the substitutes and high-bounty men, of which the 28th received a great many in 1863 and 1864, were much worse. These new recruits included hopeless cripples, lunatics, thieves, and scoundrels of every sort. Such men were hardly worth the trouble it took to bring them into camp. The regiment's monthly report for July shows that Lt. James B. West, Lt. James A. McIntyre, and

Capt. Jeremiah W. Coveney had all been sent to Massachusetts to bring out the new conscripts. Catton, *Army of the Potomac*, III 23–30; Mass. War Records.

In camp at Morrisvill Va   August the 10th 63

My dear wife

I received your verry welcome letter yesterday   I was begining
to feel very uneasy at being so long without hearing from you   I
am verry sorry to hear that your health continues so poor   i wish
you would get some place to board out of the citty for a few weeks
it would do you a great deal of good   you can not expect to get
board in such a place for less then three dollars a week   You say
that you see there is another great battle coming off   you need not
be uneasy for there is no prospect of any fighting for some time
we moved our camp since i last wrote and it is expected that we will
remain here for six or eight weeks   that at least is the present
intention of our comanding General   we will remain here untill
the conscripts are brought out and drilled sufficient to enable them
to go through their pacings and handle their arms   that will give
us a good rest   this is the program unless it is changed by Lee
asuming offensive opperations which i do not think he will be able
to do verry soon   If you have them articles bought that you intended to send to me you might send them by express   i will be
shure to get it if we remain here   if you send anything be shure to
send some tobaco   it is very dear here   plug cavendish is what i
want   if you have not any of the articles bought you had better
not mind them but if you are sending them get a small box and
put them in and nail it up   you could get a small box at a grocery
store that would suit   I do not want any mony   i can get along
untill we get paid which we expect to very soon   I had a hard
job to read Sarahs[1] letter   she writes so cramped but i made it out
do not neglect to write to them soon and i will write to them again
i want you to send me Franks[2] letter   if he has got any such notion
as you say i think i can put it out of his head when i write again
a discription of the horrors of war and the hardships and sufferings
to be endured by men in the field would i think be likely to change
his mind   i would be very sorry if anything that i wrote should be
the cause of making him think of leaving his parents and his home
he is young and probebly full of enthusiasm which is no sighn of
a want of comen sense in a young person   i would much rather see
him enthusastic then defecient of it   Give love to them all when

you write and tell them that i will write to them soon   I wish you would write to my sister mary[3] and let them know that i am well they must be uneasy about me   Give my love to all our friends and let me know in your next how they are all getting along   And now my dear wife i must conclude   may God grant you health of body and peace of mind and protect us both and bring us happy together again

Your loving husband
PETER WELSH

1. Sarah Prendergast, sister of Margaret Welsh.
2. Francis Prendergast, brother of Margaret Welsh.
3. Cannot further identify.

In camp at Morrisvill   August 21st/63

My dear wife

I received your welcome letter on yesterday   i hope you will feel better after you move up town   it is healthier   We got two months pay on the fifteenth   i sent you twenty dollars by express I hope the box will come safe   it will be quite a treat   it is better the books did not come   i could not take care of them when we moved but i am just as much oblidged to John[1] as if i got them   We have had very hot weather since we came here   we have our tents all covered with green boughs to shade of [off] the sun   there is some reports that we are going to move soon back towards Alexandria it is said but i think it all depends on how matters go at Charleston[2]   if our forces capture it the rebs will be compelled to abandon all Virginia north of Richmond or elce bring all the force they have here and make their last desperate strugle   i hope to God that Charleston will be captured soon for the war would have to come to an end very soon after   We expect a lot of conscripts to our regiment in a few days   we will have no fighting here under present sircumstances   there has been a good many troops taken from this army of late   all the regular troops that were in this army are gone so that we are not in a condition to fight untill the regiments are filled up   Let me know in your next what James Burns is doing   Give my love to all enquiring friends   do not neglect writing as soon as you get this   If i get the box before i get another letter from you i will write and let you know   Good by   God bless and protect you

Your loving husband
PETER WELSH

1. Cannot identify.

2. The capture of Charleston, South Carolina had been a Union objective since the war had begun there in April 1861. A year later a fleet of Federal ironclads had been repulsed by heavy Confederate fire from the forts and batteries ringing the harbor. From July to September 1862 the Union tried again with a joint army–navy force. Despite their capture of Morris Island and reduction of Fort Sumter to a pile of rubble, the city continued to hold out. It did not fall until Sherman cut its

supply lines from the rear on his march through South Carolina in February 1865. Bruce Catton, *The Centennial History of the Civil War,* III: *Never Call Retreat* (Garden City, N.Y.: Doubleday, 1965), 122–32, 217–26, 433–34.

Camp of the 28th Mass Voll
Morrisvill   August 28th/63

My dear wife

I received the box day before yesterday   i would have wrote rite away but i expected a letter from you   i wrote to you a week ago   i sent you twenty dollars on the 15th   we got two months pay The box had been opened but all you sent came safe   the provost guard open all boxes to search for liquor as it is not alowed come to any soldier   there was the tobaco pipe the cheese prayer book paper envelopes penholder two towls one poket handerchief two bottles of pickles and two combs and ink bottle   All the articals you sent were just what suited and they are twice as good to me on acount of you having sent them   tell Ann Gleason that i am verry thankfull to her for the pipe   i [it] is a good one and i will often remember the giver when i am smoking it   We got a lot of conscripts last sunday   they are nearly [all] New Yorkers who went to Boston and came out as substitutes   a great many of them have been out before in two years regiments   there was about two hundred came altogether   They are a wild lot of fellows with plenty of mony some of them got from four to five hundred dollars for coming   I will write a letter to frank in a few days and you can send it for me[1]   My dear wife i hope you are getting better health   i wish this war was over so that i could go home to you and nothing but death should seperate us again   i am well and hearty thank God   give my love to all our friends   good by and God bless and protect you

your loving husband
PETER WELSH

1. Margaret's brother, Francis Prendergast, was still living in Ireland at this time, but he came to New York in April of 1864. See letter of April 29, 1864.

Camp of the 28th Regiment Mass Voll
Morrisvill   September 9th/63

My dear wife

I received your letter of August 23d in due time   i had sent a
letter to you on the evening before   we had to go away on the day
after down to U S Ford on picket and were away five days   the
whole core went so when we got back i expected a letter from you
every day but i have got none since   I cannot hear anything of the
Corcorn Legion[1]   they have not joined this core as yet   i would
like to see John Burns[2]   I did not know who Cpt Lawler[3] was before i spoke to him about it since he has been in command of the
regiment for [only] the last month   the Colonel and Major have
both been away on furlow[4]   My dear wife i never felt so home sick
as since i have been in this camp and i feel it most on your acount
you get such bad health and you are so lonesome   God grant that
we may soon be together again   keep up your courage   we will be
all right yet   I will not write any more this time as i expect a letter
from you to day or tomorrow   God bless and protect you

your loving husband
PETER WELSH

1. The Corcoran Legion was a brigade composed primarily of Irish-
Americans raised by Gen. Michael Corcoran in late 1862. When it later
joined the Army of the Potomac it consisted of the 155th, 164th, 170th,
and 182nd New York infantry regiments. Boatner, *Dictionary*, p. 176.

2. There was a Maj. John Byrne in the 155th New York, one of the
regiments in the Corcoran Legion, to whom Welsh might be referring,
but no connection between this Irish-born soldier from Buffalo and
Peter Welsh can be established. Phisterer, *New York in the War*, V
3809. Though there is nothing in the context to suggest it, this could
also be a reference to John Burns, "The Old Hero of Gettysburg." This
Burns, a 70-year-old resident of Gettysburg, became a national hero
when he took up a musket and fought with the Union forces from July
1 to 3, 1863. Although badly wounded, captured by the Confederates,
and almost hanged as a spy, Burns survived and enjoyed his celebrity
status until death claimed him in 1872. *Appletons' Cyclopaedia*.

3. Capt. Andrew J. Lawler was a 26-year-old brass finisher from Bos-

ton when he received his commission in the 28th on October 8, 1861. He was promoted to major shortly after this letter (Sept. 21, 1863), but was killed in action May 18, 1864 at the battle of Spotsylvania. *Mass. Soldiers*, III 221.

4. Capt. E. H. Fitzpatrick noted that Col. Richard Byrnes and Maj. Andrew P. Caraher were "absent sick" when he filled out the 28th's monthly report on August 31, 1863. 28th Massachusetts Monthly Report for August 1863, Mass. War Records.

September the 19th/63   Near Culpeper Va

My dear wife

I received your welcome letter of the 13th on last night   we broke camp on this day week   we are laying near the Rapidan our Cavelry drove the ememy from near the Rapahanoc untill they crossed the Rapidan   our Core up here to support the Cavelry so that they do all the fighting and skirmishing and we lay behind to support them in case the enemy should try to outflank them and atack them in force   My dear wife you wished me to let you know if i got two months pay before the last that i did not send you any of   i did get two months pay just before we started from Falmouth last spring   i meant to mention it to you but i must have forgotten it when writing in a hury on the march   i kept that pay as we were going on a hard campaighn and i did not know what might happen to me in case i should be taken sick on the march or be taken prisoner   i would be badly off without money   besides on long and forced marches and in time of battle it often happens that our suply wagons can not come up and we may be left without food but if a man has mony about him he can buy bread and milk from farmers in a great many places   i kept the whole of that then because i did not know how long it might be before we would get paid again   besides in hot weather you do not know what a treat it is to a man here to get some milk or a bit of butter when they have been weeks and months perhaps without tasting anything but hard bread and salt pork and coffe with once in a while a little fresh beef   no vegetables nothing but the same old thing over and over again   such is nesessarly the case when an army is on the march or when fighting is going on   of course we get other things when we are in camp but not on the march   My dear wife you need not be afraid that i am getting reckless nor that i am turning to fret   i put my trust in God and take things as they come   My dear wife you say i ought to get $34 instead of $26 per two month but i do not draw sergeants pay yet although i am a sergeant by rank i explained to you before how it was   there can not be more then five sergeants in a company and there is five before me still on the pay roll of my company   one has been absent in hosptal over a year and we do not know where he is   the Captain expected he was discharged when i was promoted or if he wasent that he should either return to his company or not draw sergeants pay[1]   another one that was wounded at the battle of Fredericksburg was so badly wounded that he never will be able to do duty in his company   but he has not been discharged yet[2]   however it is but right that he should draw the pay as long as he can for he is disabled   my captain intends to see after the other fellow who never got wounded but went to hospital sick and never wrote to his regiment since to let them know where he was   but just at that time that trouble comenced between the Colonel and company officers about his bringing strange officers into the regiment and my Captain was the leader of it   he put him under arest and kept him under arest untill a short time before we left falmouth   when he got his trial and was released from arest he resighned and went home so there was no one to look after the matter as our company was left then without any officer but a young fellow who was not long promoted a second Leutenant[3]   so the matter stands   My dear wife you need not be afraid me being reduced to the ranks   i never got into any trouble nor got into any disgrace nor receved a single reprimand from an officer since i joined the regiment   I will write that letter to frank as soon as we get settled again   give my love to all our friends   God bless and protect you

your loving husband
PETER WELSH

1. 1st Sgt. David T. Powers. See note 4 to letter of May 7, 1863.

2. This is probably a reference to Andrew H. Doyle who was wounded severely at Fredericksburg and never rejoined the regiment. In January of 1864 he was finally transferred to the Veteran Reserve Corps. Doyle had been a Milford, Massachusetts bootmaker before the war. *Mass. Soldiers*, III 261.

3. James A. McIntyre was a "morocco dresser" from Lynn when he enlisted in the 28th as a corporal on September 20, 1861. He received his commission as second lieutenant December 14, 1862. He made captain before he was killed May 5, 1864 at the battle of the Wilderness. *Mass. Soldiers*, III 196.

In Camp near Rapidan Station Va
September 25th/63

My dear wife

I sent you a letter on the nineteenth   i received yours of thirteenth the day previous   We received two months pay yesterday i sent you $20 twenty dollars   i will be able to send you thirty next pay as i will draw sergeants pay from the first of this month   that has been settled   that sergeant who had been absent so long without hearing from him has been droped from the rolls and i draw the pay instead of him[1]   We have been laying still here eight days   our men doing picket at the river every fourth day   the enemys picket line is between three and four miles from here   we donnot know what hour we may move but it is pretty certain that our Generals do not intend to atack the enemy in front of where we ar for they have a very strong position on a range of hills on the south side of the Rapidan   if General Meade[2] makes an attack it will be on either flank   our Cavelry have had considerable skirmishing with the enemy on our right for some days past   i think our movements here depend on the result of Rosecrans[3] battle with Brag[4] in Georgia   we have received no reliable information here yet of the final result of that battle[5]   My dear wife i have nothing of much interest to write you at present   i hope to have a letter from you very soon I am hearty and well thank God   i hope with his blessing that you are getting better health   Give my love to all our friends   God bless and protect you

Your loving husband
PETER WELSH

1. 1st Sgt. Powers was dropped from the 28th's rolls as a deserter on September 1, 1863. See note 4 to letter of May 7, 1863.

2. Gen. George Gordon Meade (1815–1872) commanded the Army of the Potomac from June 28, 1863 until the end of the war, though his powers were limited after March 12, 1864 by the fact that the commander of all the Union forces, General Grant, decided to accompany the army in its campaigns against Lee. Meade was born in Spain of American parents and educated at West Point (1835). Primarily a topographical engineer before the war, he spent most of his time surveying

railroad lines and boundaries and in the design and construction of lighthouses. When the war broke out he was named brigadier general of volunteers through the influence of Gov. Andrew G. Curtin of Pennsylvania. His able command of the Fifth Corps at Chancellorsville recommended him for the army's command after Lincoln accepted Hooker's resignation in June 1863. Meade was an able commander who always remained loyal to Grant, despite the difficult situation created by his superior's decision to share battlefield control of his army. *DAB*.

3. Gen. William Starke Rosecrans (1819–1898) was commander of the Union Army of the Cumberland from October 1862 until October 1863. Rosecrans graduated from West Point in 1842 and served as an army engineer until he resigned his commission in 1854 to take advantage of business opportunities in civilian life. He returned to the army when the war broke out and rose to command the Army of the Cumberland, defeating Gen. Braxton Bragg's Army of Tennessee at the battle of Stone's River, for which he was breveted major general. His later defeat by Bragg at Chickamauga ended his career as a field officer. Called "Old Rosey" by the men, Rosecrans was popular with the army, but his hot temper often brought him into conflict with his superiors. *DAB*.

4. Gen. Braxton Bragg (1817–1876) was commander of the Confederate Army of Tennessee from June 1862 until December 1863. Born in North Carolina and educated at West Point (1837), Bragg served with distinction in the Mexican War. When the Civil War broke out he was a Louisiana planter, but he returned to the army and rose quickly in the Confederate service due to his energy and vigor. His lack of persistence and unwillingness to exploit his victories were his undoing, however, and his close friend Jefferson Davis was finally forced to remove him from command of the Army of Tennessee after his defeat at Chattanooga (Nov. 23–25, 1863). *DAB*.

5. The battle of Chickamauga (Sept. 19–20, 1863) between Gen. Bragg's Army of Tennessee and Gen. Rosecrans' Army of the Cumberland was a decided southern victory, though Bragg's failure to follow up his success with an energetic pursuit of his defeated foe robbed the South of the fruits of that victory. The defeated Union forces besieged by Bragg in Chattanooga were resupplied and reinforced over the next two months. And, at the battle of Chattanooga (Nov. 23–25, 1863), they broke out of the city and drove Bragg south into Georgia. The Confederacy lost control of a main east–west link and the stage was set for Sherman's advance into Georgia.

In camp near Brandy station
October the 7th/63

My dear wife

I received your welcome letter of the twenty seventh of Sept in due time   the reason i did not answer it before this was that i sent you twenty dollars on the twentythird and wrote you a letter the same time   so that kept me waiting expecting one from you in answer to it every day but i received none as yet   My dear wife you think it is time that i got a furlow but there is no chance untill winter   there is no furlows granted now but i will do my best to get one as soon as we get into winter quarters   My dear wife you have been missinformed about Suttlers being alowed to sell licquor here   They are not alowed to sell it to inlisted men but they were alowed to sell it to officers untill lately   but they are not alowed to bring it here under any pretence now unless they can smugle it in of course they used to sell it to soldiers when they had it for the big profit made from the price they sold it at was to strong a temtation for for [sic] a Suttler to resist   but by selling to soldiers their whole stock horses tent wagons and every thing they had were liable to be conviscated and themselves sent outside the line with orders not to return again   that is the Provost Marshals buisness and i have seen it done with several Suttlers   they are a lot of extortioners and find few to pitty them when they are dropped on   We [had] cases of this in our brigade quite lately but they were not sutlers   one was a woman that cooked for Colonel Kelly[1] who is acting Brig'r General   her husband is a private in the 88th and she has been with him ever since the brigade came out   she managed in some way to get licquor and used to put in about half water and then sell it for five dollars a canteen which holds about three pints   she was sent to prison at Washington   the other case was a man who took care of Colonel Kellys horses   he played the same game but was caught and courtmartialed   i have not heard what his sentence is yet   Licquor is ocasionly isued to the men by orders of division generals and and [sic] i strongly suspect that through the disonesty of the comissery department they got the whisky that was ordered for us and sold it as as [sic] i have described   of course the comisery have a large share of the enormas proffits   My dear wife we have a priest continualy with us   father Corbit of the 88th is always with us where ever we go and always ready to do anything he can for any one of the brigade[2]   I had quite a surprise this morning   Dudly Burns[3] came to se me   i did not know that he was in this core as you mentioned that he went to the same regiment with his brother   he is in the 42nd [N]Y   They are in the second division of this core   i would of seen him before but they were not in the same place with us when we were out in front   this core has been relieved from the front   we came back here yesterday   i do not know how long we will remain here   the general belief is that we are going to do railroad guard some where between Culpepper and Alexandria   this place is about half way between Culpepper and the Rapahanock   I hope to hear from yo soon   do not delay writing when you get this   give my love to all our friends God bless and protect you

> your loving husband
> PETER WELSH

Adress your letter

> Sargeant Peter Welsh Co K
> 28th Mass Volls 2nd Brigade
> 1st Division 2nd Corps
> Washington D.C.

1. Col. Patrick Kelly, born in Galway, Ireland, served briefly as captain in the 69th New York State Militia and in the 16th U.S. Infantry before joining the 88th New York Volunteers. He was commissioned lieutenant colonel on September 14, 1861 and colonel on October 20, 1862. Colonel Kelly assumed command of the Irish Brigade May 14, 1863 when General Meagher resigned. He was killed in action June 16, 1864 at Petersburg. Heitman, *Historical Register*, I 590; Conyngham, *Irish Brigade*, p. 558.

2. Rev. William Corby, C.S.C.

3. Dudley Byrnes was the brother of James E. Byrnes and was also a close friend of Margaret and Peter Welsh. He was only 19 when he enlisted in the 42nd New York as a private on September 11, 1863. Byrnes

made sergeant and served with the 82nd and the 59th New York infantry regiments before being discharged for disability on February 18, 1865. Adjutant-General, State of New York, *Annual Report of the Adjutant-General of the State of New York for the Year 1900* (Albany: Lyon, 1901), p. 907.

In Camp near Brandy station   October 19/63

My dear wife

I received your welcom letter of the fifth yesterday   i am very sorry to hear that you have been so sick   i hope with Gods blessing that you are better before this   My dear wife i enjoy the best of health thank God   i do not know what it is to feel sick now   It is useless for you to expect me to get a furlow now   there is no chance untill we get into winter quarters but when we do i will do my best to get one   I seen Dudly Burns yesterday   he wonders that he does not get a letter   he wrote two and got no answer   his regiment is camped close beside us   he is in good health   I sent you a letter on the 8th   i expect we will move from here verry soon   I have not much to [write] this time   there is nothing new transpiring here   My dear wife i know you must feel verry lonsome when you are sick with no one to take care of you or comfort you   God grant that i may soon be with you again   be of good cheer   God is good   May his blessing be with you

Your loving husband
PETER WELSH

Why dont you send me your adress of where you live and then there would be no delay in getting my letters[1]

1. Margaret was evidently planning to "live out" for a time, though it may have been quite a while until she actually left her uncle's. On February 1, 1864, Peter is still inquiring whether she is "at Mr. Coulter's yet?"

In camp near Cattel [Catlett's] station Va   November the 2nd/63

My dear wife

I received your welcome letter day before yesterday   i would of answered it sooner but i did not have a bit of paper to write on   i lost what i had and there was not a sheet of paper to be had around here   I never got the letter you sent before this   My dear wife there is no danger of their keeping longer then the term of the regiment   i know they kept some of the two years men and some were discharged with their regiment   it depends on their conditions of enlistment but all the recruits that came to 3 years regiments enlisted on the condition that they were to be discharged with their regiment[1]   My dear wife you talk of going to Ireland   i often thought since i been out here that it would be the best thing you could do to take a trip home to Ireland   it would do your health more good then anything you could do   it would be a great change for you and would cheer you up to see your own family and friends again   but i would feel it verry lonsome as i could not hear from you near so often and your letters are the only comfort i have although they always bring me trouble of mind and sorrow because of the fretted and unhappy way you are   you did not say anything about your health   i hope it is better   i have been unwell myself for eight or ten days past but i am quite well again thank God   i had dioarhoae first and then a bad cold   My dear wife i will try my best to get a furlow the first chance after we go into winter quarters   Write as soon as you get this   i will write to you soon again i will also write home before long   give my love to all our friends God bless and Protect you

your loving husband
PETER WELSH

I seen Dudly Burns a few days ago   he was well   he said he had not received any letter from home yet

1. See note 5 to letter of February 22, 1863.

In camp near Kellys ford Va
November the 13th/63

My dear wife

I received your welcome letter of the seventh to day   i sent you a letter on the sixth   We have had a move since   we broke camp on last saturday morning and marched to Kellys ford   there was considerable skirmishing but our corps was not engaged in any of it[1] our army drove the enemy across the Raphahanoc saturday and we crossed over sunday morning and advanced to our present Position i do not know how many priosoners was captured   i have not seen any papers since as our Regiment is away from the rest of the Division   we are doing provost guard duty   it is a good job if we are continued at it but i do not know whether we will or not   There is a report here that General Meagher has taken comand of the brigade again and that he is going to get it home to recruit it up but how much truth there is in it i can not say[2]   i hope it is true and that our regiment may go with the rest of the brigade   we would have a good time for the winter   My dear wife you did not mention in your letter how your health was   be shure to let me know in your next   i am in excelant health thank God   I seen Dudly burns five days ago   he is well   he told me that he received a letter My dear wife you need not send me any money   i expect we will get paid soon   Give my love to all our friends   God bless and protect you

your loving husband
PETER WELSH

1. On November 7th Meade's army crossed the Rappahannock at Rappahannock Station and Kelly's Ford, engaging Lee severely at both places. The army continued to move forward on the 8th as Lee withdrew to the Rapidan. It was not a major offensive, but it restored the positions that had existed before the recent Bristoe campaign (October 9–22) in which Lee had gone on the offensive to take advantage of the Federal reduction in force caused by sending troops west to take part in the Chattanooga campaign. Long, *Civil War Day by Day*, pp. 431, 419.

2. The Boston *Pilot* of November 21, 1863 also reported the rumor, but it proved false. Although Meagher's resignation as brigadier general

was canceled December 23, 1863, he did not rejoin the brigade. In fact, he was not given orders to report for duty until September 13, 1864 when he was told to proceed to Nashville and report to Gen. William Tecumseh Sherman. Athearn, *Meagher,* pp. 131–33.

In camp near Kellys ford Va   Nbr 25th/63

My dear wife

I received your welcome letter day before yesterday   We got paid last week   i sent you $30.00 thirty dollars which i expect you will get by the time you get this letter   We are still on provost duty here but i expect we will move very soon as we must move some where before the winter rain sets in   Mr Cartwright[1] is leutenent Colonel of this regiment   he was promoted a year ago   i spoke to him about Mr Coulter[2]   he says he is an intimate friend of his   he told me to send his best wishes to him   My dear wife you wish i could get promoted so that i could resighn   i wish i was promoted but a man will never get promoted if they think he intends to resighn   but i have no friends to do anything for me in the regiment   there is no one in the regiment that ever knew me at home and it is the influence of friends that gets men promoted here   if i had anyone at home to use their influence with the Colonel or leut Colonel i would stand a good chance   there is one thing certain that i know i am more competent to fill an officers position then more then one half of the officers that are in the regiment   Andrew Lawler is Major now   Caraher[3] was major but he got transfered to the inveliede core[4]   Lawler was senior captain that is how he got it although there is other captains in the regiment twice more fit for the position then him   I received James Burns letter   i would answer it but i have no paper and there are no sutlers here   i will write him a long letter as soon as i get paper   i want to find out about that leutenent   he is discharged   i am sending his adress on a slip of paper in this letter   i got his adress from an officer of the 81st   I will [write] a letter home as soon as i can   i have not seen Dudly burns since i last wrote   And now my dear wife i must conclude   May God bless and protect you

Your loving husband
PETER WELSH

1. George W. Cartwright was a Boston printer when he was mustered into the 28th as a major on December 24, 1861. He was later promoted to lieutenant colonel, was wounded at Second Bull Run and

the Wilderness, and was mustered out with the regiment December 19, 1864. *Mass. Soldiers*, III 190.

2. A Mr. and Mrs. Coulter employed Margaret Welsh as a domestic, but nothing further is known of this Coulter family.

3. Captain Caraher was promoted to major in July 1862, but wounds received at Chantilly (Sept. 1, 1862) and Fredericksburg (Dec. 13, 1862) disabled him sufficiently to require his transfer to the Veteran Reserve Corps (Invalid Corps—see next note) on September 20, 1863. *Mass. Soldiers*, III 193.

4. The Invalid Corps (later known as the Veteran Reserve Corps) to which Welsh refers was an organization of soldiers who were unfit for combat duty, but who could perform limited duty so that able-bodied soldiers could be released for duty in the field. Men in the corps were employed as guards, clerks, hospital attendants, nurses, and cooks. Special sky-blue uniforms were created for the corps. Corps members continued to receive the regular pay and allowances of infantrymen, but were ineligible for any pensions or bounties for their enlistment. Lord, *They Fought for the Union*, p. 64.

In camp near Stevensburg Va
December 18th/63

My dear wife

I received your welcome letter of the 4th in due time   i should have answered it sooner but i was expecting another letter from you every day but did not get it yet   i wrote you a letter on the 3d the day after we got back from the other side of the Rapidan and got no answer to it yet[1]   We moved a short distance since i wrote we got into the woods and we have been busy building winter quarters   we have not got them all finished yet   My dear wife i have got the promise of a furlow but i can not get it yet a while as there was some who had applied for furlows last winter and did not get them and they have to get the first chance   there is four of them gone   there will be another lot to go before me   There is an order here for reinlisting old hands for three years   there is a good many of them say they will reinlist   they get about seven hundred dollars bounty and thirty days furlow right away   if there is three quarters of them reinlist they will go home as a regiment   if not the regiment will be kept up here[2]   how it will be i can not tell yet but i hope to get my furlow some time next month   Colonel Burns[3] has gone to New York on a furlow of 30 days   he lives in Brooklyn I seen Dudly Burns a few days ago   he had heard of his fathers death   i am very sorry for their trouble   My dear wife i must conclude now   i will write to you again in a few days   i hope to get one from you in a day or two   give love to all our friends   God bless and protect you

your loving husband
PETER WELSH

1. This letter cannot be located. It is likely that Margaret never received it as Peter notes in his letter of December 31, 1863 that she never acknowledged receipt of the letter. It probably contained an account of his recent experiences in the Mine Run campaign from which the brigade had just returned. The Army of the Potomac crossed the Rapidan on November 26th and moved to Mine Run, Virginia. But Meade, finding Lee's position too strong to attack, had the army recross the river and return to camp on December 1–2. The 28th Massachusetts

suffered its only casualties in the campaign on November 29th in a skirmish near Robinson's Tavern. Boatner, *Dictionary*, p. 552; Conyngham, *Irish Brigade*, p. 579.

2. General Orders No. 191 of the Adjutant General's Office of the War Department, issued June 25, 1863, provided that veteran volunteers re-enlisting for three years or the duration of the war were entitled to a bounty of $402 and a thirty-day furlough after their original term of enlistment expired. General Order No. 33 of the Adjutant General of Massachusetts, issued November 21, 1863, provided an additional bounty of $325 to veterans re-enlisting in Massachusetts regiments. Section V of General Orders No. 376 of the Adjutant General's Office of the War Department provided that when three-fourths of any company or regiment re-enlisted they could go home as a body on their furloughs to reorganize and recruit. *OR*, ser. III, vol. 3, pp. 414–16; Mass. War Records; *OR*, ser. III, vol. 3, p. 1084.

3. This may be a reference to Col. Richard Byrnes of the 28th, but if it is, Welsh is mistaken about his place of residence. Byrnes lived in Jersey City, New Jersey at this time. Richard Byrnes Pension File, NA.

In camp near Stevensburg Va
December the 31st/63

My dear wife

I received your welcome letter of the 25th in due time   i was verry uneasy at not hearing from you for so long   you did not mention whether you received my second last letter or not   i wrote it the day after we got back from the other side of the rapidan   that was the second of the month   i was waiting for an answer to that before i wrote my last letter   My dear wife i am afraid that i will not be able to get a furlow this winter   there has been an order isued that no furlows be granted except to those who reinlist   i feel very much disapointed   i hoped to get home to see you some time this winter   This regiment expected to get home   nearly all the old hands reinlisted but an order came out that a regiment could not go home unless the three fourths of their whole number present reinlisted   there is not enough old hands in the regiment present for that so they had to give it up   we got so many substitutes is what stops the regiment from going   there is very few who will reinlist indivedualy as the regiment cant go[1]   I am in hopes that there may be a chance to get a furlow yet this winter after this reinlisting is done with   if i cant get home i must only content myself the best i can untill next fall and then please God i will have a long furlow   My dear wife i would like to have some little things from home but i do not want you to go to the expense for my pay will be small for this two months   i am in debt for clothing   we are alowed $42 dollars per year for clothing   that will keep any man who takes care of his cloths well clad if he does not loose them   but i lost a goodeal of clothing since i enlisted and i got to settle up to the first of the new year [for] clothing that we packed up and sent away last spring and never got it again   we had to draw others in place of them and now we are charged for them   if it hadent been for that and some i lost in action i would of come out right enough it is a great wrong that men should have to pay for clothing lost in this way and we wouldent have to pay for them if the comander of the regiment would look after it   If you should wish to send me a few articals in in [sic] a box any time you can direct it to Patrick Nolan 1st Leut Co K 28th Mass Vols   by sending it in his name the

139

box will not be opened and you can send anything you like in it all that would be necessary would be to write a note and put it in the box stating who it was for   I am not in need of any clothing we get stockings from the government cheaper then you could buy them at home 32 cents a pair   the thing i am most defeciant of is gloves   i have none   i bought a pair of boots   i also had gloves but lost them in the fall campaighn   My dear wife we have got our winter quarters built   we are pretty comfortable considering where we are   we have small houses built   four men in each house   the roof covered with four pieces of shelter tents   they are dry and warm   I hope you spent Christmas pleasent   i spent it very dull   there was nothing to be got here   even the sutlers were unable get up anything for Christmas   i seen Dudly Burns on Christmas day   he came over to see me   he is well   I had a letter from James Burns a few days ago   i will write to him in a few days My dear wife i must now conclude by wishing heave[n']s choisest blessings on you

Your loving husband
PETER WELSH

Give my love to all our friends   i wish them all a happy new year

---

1. The 28th Massachusetts eventually had 157 re-enlisted "Veteran Volunteers," of which Peter Welsh was one. *Mass. Adj.-Gen.* (1866), p. 13. See illustration.

1864

"WE LICKED SAUCEPANS OUT OF THEM"

ON THE LAST DAY OF 1863 Peter Welsh was discharged from the 28th Massachusetts so he could re-enlist in the regiment on the first day of the new year. He was entitled to a large bounty from both the state and federal governments for doing so, but his action does not seem to be motivated by money. More important was the furlough all veterans received who were willing to re-enlist "for three years or during the war." For a long time he had wanted to go home to see Margaret, and she, it appears from his letters, was getting desperate to see him. She even talked of coming down to Stevensburg, Virginia, where the Army of the Potomac was in winter quarters, to be with him. But Peter reminded her that he would be home soon, and begged her, "for God's sake do not think of coming out here!" Welsh finally got his furlough and arrived in New York on February 27, 1864. He was home for 35 days, but, as he later told his father-in-law, "the time slipped by on lightning wheels."

When he rejoined his regiment in early April, the Army of the Potomac was gearing up for a spring offensive with a new man in charge. While General Meade was ostensibly still at the helm, Lt. Gen. Ulysses S. Grant had decided to accompany the army and direct Meade's operations. The eastern theater was in for a new kind of warfare, for Grant was not one to retreat after a loss or fail to follow up a victory. Whatever happened, Grant was determined to move on Richmond and force Lee's army to slug it out with him every step of the way. Both armies would fight until one of them was destroyed.

On May 3rd the army broke camp and crossed the river into the Wilderness where Hooker had come to grief the year before. In rapid succession the Federals engaged the Army of Northern Virginia at the Wilderness, Po River, and Spotsylvania Court House. Day after day they fought and day after day they moved south. At the Wilderness alone Welsh's regiment lost 119 men, but they moved on. While the North waited for word from the front and anxious families scanned the long casualty lists, Margaret heard nothing from Peter. Finally, a letter arrived. It was dated May 15th and was written from Carver Hospital in Washington. It was the last letter Margaret received from her husband, but it was characteristically buoyant. He dismissed the severity of the wound he had received at Spotsylvania on May 12th and exulted in the army's success on that day. It "was the greatest battle of the war," he told Margaret; "we licked saucepans out of them!"

In camp near Stevensburg Va   January 12th/64

My dear wife

I received your welcome letter of the 5th on yesterday   I would
have wrote to James Burns but i am scarcely able to scrible atall   i
have got a fellon on my thumb and it is with great difficulty that i
can hold a pen[1]   it is getting better and i will soon be able to use
it again   My dear wife you write wildly about coming out here
you do not know the difficulties you would have to contend with
it is verry different from the Corcaran Legion   they are close by a
railroad and a town   we are miles away from the railroad and it
would be impossible for you to find our camp without some one to
direct you when you arrived at brandy station   you should leave
the cars and how would you know which way to go   there would
be miles to travel through mud and slush knee deep   how would
you feel wandering through a strange wild country where there is
no hospitable farm house on the wayside into which you could
go for shelter or information   this is a country now from which
civilisation has taken flight   nothing left but the barren field and
wild forrest   and even could you find your way to our camp how
would it be then   there is no place i could take you except my
tent which is ocupied by three others with me   if we were near a
town or citty where you could get a place to stop a few weeks i
would encourage you to come for then you could stay there and i
could go there to see you and be with you nearly all the time for i
have nothing to do when we are in camp   but under present circumstances for Gods sake do not think of coming out here   I am
shure of getting home some time this winter and it may be verry
soon   so you may make your mind easy   i will be home to see you
at least before the last of March   this i can tell you for certain   and
now like a good girl content yourself a little while longer and i
will be with you   i will not thank you for the box untill untill [sic]
i can do so with my own tongue   I must now conclude   give my
love to all our friends   May God bless and protect you

your loving husband

PETER WELSH

1. A "felon" is an acute and painful inflammation of the deeper
tissues of a finger or toe, usually near the nail.

In camp near Stevensburg Va   January 23d/64

My dear wife

I received your welcome letter of the 14th in due time but i could not answer it before because of my sore hand   my thumb is nearly well but when it was getting better there was another fellon came on my finger which swelled and stifened my hand so that i could not write   it is better but very sore yet   I sent you a letter a few days before i got your last   i am in exelant health thank God except my hand which will soon be well   i did not get the box yet   i am expecting it every day   i am very thankfull but i cannot write my thanks to Mrs Coulter untill i can write better   this is queer scribbling but i cant help it   We got paid   i canot send mony the old way   father Corbet[1] is home with his regiment   i will sent you ten dollars in this letter and send you more in my next   I must conclude now   May God bless and protect you

your loving husband
PETER WELSH

Dudly Burns has just come in to see me   he is well

1. Rev. William Corby, C.S.C.

In camp near Stevensburg Va   January 29th/64

My dear wife

I received the box the day before yesterday   everything came safe except the brandy   some scoundrell opened the bottom of the box and took the bottle of brandy   the bottle of whisky and the bottle of bitters came safe   when i opened it and found the whisky i thought it was all safe but when i went to look for the brandy i found the mufler and nothing in it   but we had a good time on what was in it   the cake was splendid   my captain[1] and Capt Coveny[2] and Leut Nolan[3] helped me to welcome the box   they with Sergeant OShea[4] and Corporal Watson[5] who are my tent mates and myself made the whiskey and bitters and turkey leave pretty quick   I seen Dudly Burns the day before but he could not come over that day as he had to go on guard   he came over yesterday but i did not have a sup to give him   i used all the whisky and bitters before i knew that the brandy was taken out   My dear wife i have not had an answer to my last two letters   i am expecting one every day   i sent you a letter a few days ago with ten dollars in it as we got paid and father Corbat[6] is home with his regiment i had to send it that way   i have some more to send you but i do not like to send it untill i hear if that went safe   We expect to be transfered to cavelry   the papers are gone to Washington   i hope we will   we would have a horse to ride and our regiment will go home to recreut and drill   we would probebly have three or four months at home   My dear wife tell Mrs. Coulter and her sister that i cannot find words to express my gratitude for their kindness not only for the presents they sent me but more especialy for their kindness to you   that above all things touches my heart and will leave on it a mark of gratitude that can never be efaced   May God reward them with a thousand blessings for every ray of happiness they confer on my poor little wife who is so lonely and sad in my absence   i hope i will soon have a chance to thank them in person for their kindness   Colonel Cartright has gone home on furlow he got hurt by a fall from a horse   he has not spoken of anything to me since i asked him about Mr Coulter   i supose he will remain in New York while he is on furlow   My dear wife i must now

conclude   i hope to hear from you soon   May God bless and protect you

your loving husband
PETER WELSH

give my love to all our friends

    1. Capt. James A. McIntyre.

    2. Capt. Jeremiah W. Coveney.

    3. 1st Lt. Patrick Nolan.

    4. Daniel O'Shea was a Milford, Massachusetts bootmaker when he enlisted in the 28th as a corporal in September 1861. He made sergeant when he re-enlisted January 1, 1864, but was wounded at Deep Bottom on July 27th and died two days later. *Mass. Soldiers*, III 264.

    5. Peter Watson was a laborer from Roxbury, Massachusetts when he enlisted in the 28th on October 3, 1861. He made corporal when he re-enlisted January 1, 1864. He finally attained the rank of sergeant before he was mustered out June 30, 1865. *Mass. Soldiers*, III 265.

    6. Rev. William Corby, C.S.C.

In camp near Stevensburg Va   February 1st/64

My dear wife

I received your welcome letter of the twentyseventh night before last   I sent you a letter a few days before to tell you that i got the box   I did not send any mony in my last   i was waiting to hear if the other went safe   i will send ten dollars in this   My dear wife you ask if i could not get a furlow on my sore hand   it is not so easy to get a sick furlow as that   my hand is nearly well all but the nail of my thumb which i will loose   My dear wife i am in great hopes that i will see you very soon   if we get changed into Cavelry we will go home to recreuit and drill   it will take a long time before we will be fit to go to the field   i hope we may get it   cavelry have no marching to do and no fighting compared with the infantry   their principle duty is picketing and scouting on the enemys flanks   they never have to face shell shrapnel and grape and canister nor bear the slaughter of a general engagement like the infantry have   and if we do go it is not likely that we will come back to Virgenia again   and i hope not for this is a cursed state   it might well be called the sephulcher of America   Let me know in your next if you are at Mr Coulters yet   i canot tell by your letters whether you are or not   I want to know who that Mr McCormac[1] is and what he was doing out here last spring   i should like to know how he knew whether i sent you money then or not or what it was of his business   There is several more of the name of Welsh in this regiment besides me   i do not think the man knows me atall   i certainly do not know him   be shure to let me know if you can what buisness he does be on out here   Colnol Cartwright is home on furlough and Major Lawler also   i suppose you know that Lawler is maried   he lives in Gensee St Boston   Capt Fleming[2] was telling me that he was at his house when he was on furlough this winter   Let me know if you know who he is maried to   Tell me in your next how James Gleason and Ann are getting along and also how your uncle and James are doing   My dear wife i must now draw to a close   give my love to all our friends and to those from whom you have received kindness thank them for me   tell them that i will ever pray that the choicest blessings of heaven may be showered upon them and tell them that if ever an oppertunity offers where i can serve them it will be a source of the greatest happiness to me to do so they who confer a kindness on you now shall never be forgotten by me   one kind act towards you now is of more value to me then if i was the daily receipient of such favour for the whole term of my life   May they never know what it is to be seperated from those they hold dear   may they live in the posession of every blessing spiritual and temporal and when they are called from this state of probation may angels bear them on their pure wings to the throne of eternal majesty where they may adore and be happy for all eternity   Gods choisent blessings be with you

your loving husband
PETER WELSH

1. Cannot identify.

2. James Fleming was a Boston upholsterer when he enlisted as first sergeant in the 28th on October 4, 1861. He was wounded at Fredericksburg, Spotsylvania, and Hatcher's Run, but was mustered out of the regiment as a lieutenant colonel on July 19, 1865. *Mass. Soldiers,* III 203.

In camp near Stevensburg Va   February the 13th/64

My dear wife

I received your welcome letter of the seventh last night   We had a little move since i wrote last   we were on a reconaisence to the Rapidan[1]   our Division was not engagd in any of the skirmishing we were out two days   My dear wife i expect to be home to see you in a week or ten days   i will think every day a week long now untill i get home   I have not much to write as i expect to see you so soon   Give my love to all our friends   God bless and protect you

> your loving husband
> PETER WELSH

1. On February 6, 1864 Federal forces crossed the Rapidan at Morton's Ford, but were immediately pinned down by heavy Confederate fire. They withdrew north of the river that night. Long, *Civil War Day by Day*, p. 461.

In camp near Stevensburg Va   April 14th/64

My dear wife

I received yours of the tenth last night   i am very sorry to hear that you were so sick   i hope with the blessing of God that you are in better health by this   I am in excelant health thank God   i can grind hard tack and eat anything that comes the way as well as ever i could   The paymaster is here   he paid us to day   i am sending you sixty $60 dollars by Father Corbit[1] but you need not expect it for several days after you receive this letter as he can not send it untill he goes to the railroad station   My dear wife it is all false about the army moving   there is no sighns of a move here yet   it would be impossible to move in the present condition of the roads we have had a great deal of rain here lately and we are likely to have more by present appearences   I have not much news to write to you at present   That mean scoundrel of a Colonel of ours is sending out a lot more strange officers to the regiment   it is generly believed here that he has been selling comissions in Boston   some of them are men who were dismissed from the service in other regiments[2]   My dear Margaret you must not be fretting about me   i am all right now and with Gods blessing will be all right and well untill i see you again which i hope will not be verry long   I must now come to a close praying God to bless and protect you

your ever loving husband

PETER WELSH

Give my love to all our friends   tell them all if they were as happy as i wish them they would have nothing more to wish for

1. Rev. William Corby, c.s.c.

2. Of the four new lieutenants in the 28th that spring, all were from outside the regiment. Martin Binney had served in the 5th Massachusetts and the 10th Maine, Patrick W. Black had served in the 9th Massachusetts, Leonard Harvey was from the 11th Maine, and Walter J. Morgan had been in the 43rd and 56th Massachusetts infantry regiments. There may be some truth to Welsh's assertion that these officers were not all they should have been. The commission of one Jacob Nebrich was canceled before he joined the 28th, Leonard Harvey re-

signed after only a month with the regiment, and Walter J. Morgan was court-martialed and reduced to private during the summer of 1864. *Mass. Volunteers,* II 552; *Mass. Soldiers,* III 200, 243, 252, 255.

In camp near Stevensburg Va   April 25th/64

Dear father[1]

You must excuse my long neglect of writing   At the time i received Franks letter i did not have much time nor oppertunity to write and when we got into winter quarters i was waiting untill i would get home on furlow   i got home on the 27th of February and was home thirty five days   I meant to write while home but the time sliped by on lightning wheels   it seemed verry short to a man after being a year and a half from home   Margaret mentioned in the last letter i received from her that she had written to you since i was home   both of us wish very much that James[2] would come to N York   any young man of his profession can do well in this country   all that is necessary is sobriety and strict attention to his buisness   with these two qualitys any man of ordinary intilegance and ability can suceed   I feel certain that he could do much better in N York then he can at home   if i did not i would not advise him to come   he would not be coming as a stranger   he would have a home before him   he could live with Margaret   it would also be a great comfort to her to have a brother with her especialy while i am absent   He need not feel any uneasiness about means either to come or after he would come as Margaret can asist him if he wants it both before he comes and afterwards   and in case he should not find a permement situation to suit him or should not like this country and wish to return home i will guarentee that he shall not be detained for want of means to do so   My dear father and also dear mother you must not think me to medlesome in thus advising James to come to this country   i would not write to himself advising him to come but to you knowing of course that you would not oppose his going where he could best advance himself and i feel certain that his chances of advancing himself are fifty per cent greater in this country then at home   in this opinion your brother John and all our friends in N York agree with me   Tell Frank that i admire his enthusiastic spirit but to take a brotherly advice never to think of soldiering unless for free Alters and happy firesides in poor old Ireland   then indeed i would advise every man to buckle on his armour and contempt and infamy be upon the Irishman who would then prove coward or traitor   Dear father,

mother brothers and sisters i must conclude for the present by sending you all my cincerest love   May God shower down his choicest
blessings on you all   farewell for the present.

Yours affectionately
PETER WELSH

1. This letter was written to Margaret's father, Patrick Prendergast.
2. James Prendergast, brother of Margaret Welsh.

In camp near Stevensburg Va   April 29th/64

My dear wife

I received your welcome letter of the 24th last night   i am very sorry to hear that you have suffered so much with your teeth   James Byrnes did not tell me that you were so bad   you must caught cold after getting your teeth drawn   i am in excelant health thank God My dear wife i am rejoiced to hear that your brother Frank is in N York with you   i took the Cartdevisete[1] to be your Cousin Johns[2] before i read your letter   he resembles John a goodeal   i am sory he did not arrive in N York before i came away   I wrote a letter on the 25th for you to send to Ireland   you will be the best judge yourself whether to send it now or not   if you dont send it i will write another after i hear from you   I wrote to Ellen[3] on the 17th but forgot to give her the name of my regiment and company i do not know whether she knows it or not   i am waiting to hear from her before i write home   you might write to her and give my adress in case she does not know it   My dear wife write to me often   you know that after we comence marching we will often be so situated that i will not have an oppertunity to send a letter but that need not prevent you from writing   i will write to you at least once a week unless prevented for want of an oppertunity to send letters   I have nothing new to write at present   give my sincere love to all our friends   May God bless and protect you

your loving husband
PETER WELSH

1. A carte de visite was a small photograph, most commonly a portrait, mounted on a card measuring approximately 2½ by 4 inches. Cartes de visite first appeared in the United States in 1859, and by the end of the following year they had become the fashion throughout the country. They were cheaply produced, sometimes selling for as little as $1.50 a dozen, and the war, by separating men from their families, created a huge market for them. William C. Darrah, *Cartes de Visite in Nineteenth Century Photography* (Gettysburg, Pa.: Darrah, 1981), pp. 4–7, 19.

2. Cannot identify.

3. This is probably Peter's sister Ellen Welsh who was in Ireland in 1862. See letter of mid-October, 1862.

Dear brother Frank[1]

I am very glad you have come to N York i am sorry i was not there to welcome you i hope you will like N York which i think you will after you have been a few months there it is a great buisness place and just the place for a young man to embark on the sea of life it all depends on himself whether he makes a sucessful and profitable voyage or not Let me give you a few words of advice not that i believe you need it but i give it from dearly bought experiance and with sincere brotherly afection Shun the wine cup and company keeping shun the use of intoxicating drink as you would a foul and venemous serpent it is the destroyer of the happiness and prosperity of three fourths of the human race there is an old and wise proverb have but few friends and well chosen too much company keeping has led thousands of young men to their ruin The man who will shun those two vices and atend regulerly to the dutys of his relegion will be prosperous and happy no matter what his profession or abiliys may be One thing more never for heavens sake let a thought of enlisting in this army cross your mind it is right and the duty of citizens and those who have lived long enough in this country to become citizens to fight for the maintainence of law order and nationality but the country has no claim on you and never bring upon yourself the dangers and hardships of a soldiers life where the country nor cause has no claim on your service It will be a great happiness for Margaret to have you with her now do all you can to console and keep her from fretting and God reward and bless you

Your loving brother
PETER WELSH

Francis Prendergast

1. This letter, like the letter of April 25, 1864 to Margaret's father, was no doubt enclosed with Peter Welsh's April 29th letter to Margaret in New York.

Washington   May 15th/64

My dear wife

i write those few huried lines to let you know that i got slightly wounded on the 12th   it is a flesh wound in my left arm   just a nice one to keep me from any more fighting or marching this campaign   we have had a prety tough time of it   we had been 8 days constantly fighting before i got hit   that was the greatest battle of the war   we licked saucepans out of them[1]   My dear wife i think i can get sent to new york to hospital   if not i will get a sick furlow to go home   Dudly Burns has lost the first finger of his left hand James was all right when i left the front   my dear wife do not be uneasy about me   i am all right here   give my love to all our friends   God bless and protect you   write to me as soon as you get this and send me five dollars if you can   good by for the present

your loving husband

PETER WELSH

Direct your letter to Sergt Peter Welsh
Carver U S Hospital
Washington D C

1. Peter Welsh must have been wounded early in the day on the 12th if he believed that the Federals had "licked saucepans out of" Lee's army in their famous assault on the Mule Shoe Salient at Spotsylvania. At first the assault, spearheaded by Hancock's Second Corps, had been a great success. Surprising the rebels in the predawn fog, they captured twenty guns and three or four thousand Confederate infantrymen. But the day was not over. Lee himself led in reinforcements to stop the Union drive and the fighting—confused, bloody, and terrible—lasted all day and deep into the night. By the time the field fell silent sometime after midnight, the Army of the Potomac had lost nearly 7,000 casualties. One officer who lived through this awful day said, "I never expect to be fully believed when I tell what I saw of the horrors of Spotsylvania, because I would be loathe to believe it myself were the case reversed." Catton, *Army of the Potomac*, III 112–28.

Epilogue

PETER WELSH may be forgiven for believing that his wound was only a "nice one" that would keep him out of the fighting for a while. When he arrived at the Second Corps field hospital, doctors called the wound "slight" and treated it with a simple cold dressing. But two days later, when Welsh was admitted to Carver Hospital in Washington,[1] the examining surgeon O. A. Judson found that the bullet had fractured a bone in his forearm. On the 17th, Acting Assistant Surgeon J. S. Weitz removed a battered and distorted bullet and several bone fragments from his left ulna in a short operation. Up to this point Welsh was still doing well. On the 20th, however, the wound began to hemorrhage. Though pressure on the arm managed to halt the flow of blood, within a few days pyemia, a kind of blood poisoning, set in. Chills and nausea wracked Welsh's body and an "unhealthy discharge" came from the wound. He began to refuse any food or drink. By the 28th he had become delirious, and his pulse was feeble and slow. Before the day was ended Welsh's "slight wound" had taken his life.[2]

Margaret Welsh apparently rushed down to Washington to be with her wounded husband, but we cannot know for sure what passed between them in his final days since documentary evidence of her visit is sadly lacking. Army records note merely that the dead soldier's effects—a blanket, a cap, two shirts, a pair of trousers, and a pair of boots—were taken by his wife.[3] The only other evidence of her presence in Washington is a melancholy telegram she sent back to James Gleason in New York, reading simply: "HE IS DEAD AND WILL BE IN NEW YORK IN MORNING."[4] On June 1, 1864, Peter Welsh was laid to rest in Calvary Cemetery in what is today Woodside, Queens, New

York. It is fitting that his handsome monument should note the achievement that had probably given him the greatest pride his short life had known: his service as color sergeant in the Irish Brigade.[5]

Margaret lived on after the war, drawing the small pension that was due widows of Union soldiers. But her health was never very good, and in 1892, at the age of 57, she was laid to rest beside her husband in Calvary Cemetery.[6]

1. See illustration.

2. Peter Welsh Carded Medical Records, NA; George A. Otis, *The Medical and Surgical History of the War of the Rebellion*, Part II, Vol. 2, *Surgical History* (Washington, D.C.: Government Printing Office, 1877), p. 959; Peter Welsh Pension File, NA; Peter Welsh Medical Records, Armed Forces Medical Museum, Washington, D.C.

3. Peter Welsh Pension File, NA; family tradition does relate a moving story of Margaret's futile attempt to talk Peter into allowing doctors to remove his diseased arm, but the story cannot be confirmed by extant medical records. See Preface.

4. See illustration.

5. See illustration.

6. Peter Welsh Pension File, NA.

ENGAGEMENTS OF
THE 28TH REGIMENT
MASSACHUSETTS VOLUNTEER INFANTRY
4TH REGIMENT, IRISH BRIGADE

JAMES ISLAND
SECOND BULL RUN
CHANTILLY
SOUTH MOUNTAIN
ANTIETAM
FREDERICKSBURG
CHANCELLORSVILLE
GETTYSBURG
AUBURN
BRISTOE STATION
ROBINSON'S TAVERN
THE WILDERNESS
PO RIVER
SPOTSYLVANIA
NORTH ANNA
TOTOPOTOMOY
COLD HARBOR
PETERSBURG
STRAWBERRY PLAINS
DEEP BOTTOM
REAMS'S STATION
HATCHER'S RUN
SUTHERLAND STATION
SAYLER'S CREEK
FARMVILLE
APPOMATTOX

Index

abolitionists, 62, 68n, 70
Adams Express, 64
adjutant (regimental), 35, 51
Agnus Dei, 57, 58n
Ahern, John, 47, 48n
Alexandria, Va., 119, 129
ambulance corps, 46, 87, 87n, 91, 113
Andrew, John, 62, 63n, 76n
Antietam, battle of, 4, 15, 25, 26n, 28, 28n, 43
Antietam Creek, 112
Appomattox Court House, 4
Aquia Creek, 64
Army of Northern Virginia, 15, 133n, 137–38n, 141
Army of Tennessee, 127n
Army of the Cumberland, 127n
Army of the Gulf, 114n
Army of the Potomac, 15, 52–53, 53–54n, 54n, 57, 59, 59n, 60, 79, 84,
    85n, 86, 91–92n, 93, 113, 122, 133n, 137–38n, 141, 142, 150, 156n;
    Second Corps, 108–109, 110, 124, 129, 156n, 157; Third Corps, 115;
    Sixth Corps, 90, 91–92n; Ninth Corps, 69; Eleventh Corps, 91
Athy, co. Kildare, Ireland, 3
Austria, 67, 74
Averell, William Woods, 80n

Bailey, Walter S., 96n
banks, 75, 77–78
Banks, Nathaniel, 114n
Bennett, James Gordon, 30–31n
Binney, Martin, 150–51n
Black, Patrick, 150–51n
blacks, 8, 62, 63n
Bloomfield, Va., 112
Boston, Mass., 3, 4, 9, 12n, 20, 21, 24, 28, 28–29n, 35, 65, 87, 121, 147,
    150